The European Common Market and Community

THE WORLD STUDIES SERIES

VOLUMES PUBLISHED

Malaysia and its Neighbours, J. M. Gullick.

The European Common Market and Community, Uwe Kitzinger, Fellow
of Nuffield College, Oxford.

FORTHCOMING VOLUMES

John F. Kennedy and the New Frontier, Edmund Ions, Department of
History, Columbia University, New York.

Brazil: The Pattern of National Development, L. M. Bethell, University
College, London.

The Indian-Pakistan Problem, Dr. Peter Lyon, London School of
Economics.

Israel and the Arab World, C. H. Dodd, Department of Social Studies,
University of Durham.

Apartheid, Dr. Edgar Brookes.

The European Common Market and Community

UWE KITZINGER

Fellow of Nuffield College, Oxford

NEW YORK

BARNES & NOBLE, INC.

General Editor's Preface

The World Studies Series is designed to make a new and important contribution to the study of modern history. Each volume in the Series will provide students in colleges and universities with a range of contemporary material drawn from many sources, not only from official and semi-official records, but also from contemporary historical writing and from reliable journals. The material is selected and introduced by a scholar who establishes the context of his subjects and suggests possible lines of discussion and inquiry that can accompany a study of the documents.

Through these volumes the student can learn how to read and assess historical documents. He will see how the contemporary historian works and how historical judgments are formed. He will learn to discriminate among a number of sources and to weigh evidence. He is confronted with recent instances of what Professor Butterfield has called 'the human predicament' revealed by history; evidence concerning the national, racial and ideological factors which at present hinder or advance man's progress towards some form of world society.

Such is the skill with which Mr. Kitzinger has selected his documents that from their perusal the reader is helped to discern 'the line between what is actually happening today and what is hoped will be happening tomorrow in the making of Europe' (Miriam Camps, *What Kind of Europe*, page vi, London, 1965); he is invited to make up his mind about the arguments for and against British participation, and he is challenged to agree or disagree with Victor Hugo's prophecy:

> 'I represent a party which does not yet exist: Civilization. This party will make the Twentieth Century. There will issue from it, first the United States of Europe, and then the United States of the World.'

James Henderson

Contents

CONTENTS

CONTENTS

Volume Editor's Preface

There can be no such thing as an objective anthology. Any source book of the present kind—extracting a minute sample from the vast mass of economic, legal, historical and political material crying out to be included—is bound to reflect the preoccupations if not the prejudices of its editor. My prejudices are all in favour of Britain's entering into the Community if this proves possible: but these prejudices have, I imagine, been more than compensated by the extracts chosen for Part IV of this book, which dwell largely on the obstacles and objections as voiced in the debate of 1961-3. My preoccupations are with the Common Market as a political institution rather than with its economic effects: and, as the book's title indicates, it is this Community aspect to which I have given such scope as the compass of the volume allows.

Readers who are equally interested in the economic aspects of the Common Market, in the history of its relations with Britain, and in a statement of the case for British entry into the Community may be referred to my earlier *The Challenge of the Common Market* (Blackwell, Oxford, 4th edition 1962). In the present selection the emphasis is on the underlying political motivations, on the constitutional structures achieved and envisaged, and (in my final assessment) on the contribution of the Community experiment to the theory and practice of international relations.

The book was compiled in late 1965, but the publishers have been willing to add at a late stage the two documents which bring it right up-to-date: the Luxembourg compromise of January 1966 (Document 15) and Mr. Wilson's presentation of Britain's new approach to the Community (Document 24).

Standlake Manor   U.W.K.
Oxfordshire
January 1967

Acknowledgements

My gratitude is due above all to my secretary, Miss Susan Phillips, for her unfailingly efficient help at all stages in the preparation of this book.

In addition my acknowledgements are due to Messrs. Basil Blackwell for permission to draw on Chapter I of my earlier book in the first twelve pages of this one; to M. Emile Noël for his willingness to rewrite and bring up to date Document 10, and to the Conservative Political Centre and the Editors of the *Süddeutsche Zeitung* and the *Witney Gazette* for permission to republish Documents 10, 16 and 22. The translation of Document 23 is by the Press Service of the French Embassy in London, and the remaining translations by various European institutions, with the exception of Documents 1, 6 and 7 for which I must be held responsible.

U.W.K.

INTRODUCTION

1944–1950: IDEALS AND REALITIES

The political impetus for the unification of Europe effectively dates from the latter half of the Second World War. Those were the years when leading statesmen all over the world, following the principles laid down in the Allies' war aims, sought to create a far stronger League of Nations, a United Nations, even a Federation of the World. Shocked by the legal and illegal crimes against humanity which they had witnessed in the previous decade both in the pre-war dictatorships and during the war itself, appalled by the vast problems of hunger and want facing every part of the world at the end of that conflict, the World Federalist movement took as its main aim the abolition of physical force as a method of diplomacy, the abatement or abolition of the national sovereignty without which international war is impossible, and the creation of a body of international law in the full sense of the term, pronounced and sanctioned by a World Federal Authority.

The war-time negotiations that culminated in the San Francisco Conference of 1944 did not fulfil these hopes. They produced a United Nations which has certainly shown itself stronger than the old League but is still not even a confederation of states, let alone a World Government. Its General Assembly remains an assembly of Governments exercising their sovereignty—not one of representatives of the people deliberating in common for the common good. The final contradiction of the dreams of the war years was to be found in the national right to disobedience of any UN majority decision, formally recognized by the right of veto given to the five nations then regarded as big. So the hopes for a World Government were dashed to the ground.

It was soon clear that more intensive international cooperation was possible only on a less extended front. A tighter bond could only be forged between a smaller number of nations.

Failing progress on a world scale the countries of Europe (for which the federalists in Europe felt they had the most immediate responsibility) were to set an example to the world. For some idealists at least, European unity was thus not simply a regionalist approach for its own sake but a pilot project for something to come on a wider scale: any abdication of sovereignty, even on a regional basis, seemed better than allowing the nation state to consolidate itself once more after its great moral and material bankruptcy.

It was in Britain in particular that the World Federalist strain was intertwined with the ideal of European federation. The result was not entirely happy. Since federalists were among the most active in post-war relief and in international meetings, Europeans (who cannot always tell an English crank from a normal Englishman) over-estimated their strength in Britain. The moral absolutism and salvationist dogma of many of the early post-war federalists stemmed from their belief that federalism was a technical prerequisite for translating the Sermon on the Mount into practice in the twentieth century. But because in their preoccupation with ultimate aims many federalists were classified as starry-eyed, British observers were tempted to write off the federalists on the continent as equally cranky and unrepresentative. It is true that shortly after the war, the Leader of the Opposition, Mr. Winston Churchill, came out in favour of 'a kind of United States of Europe' (see Document 2, p. 33). But there was little enthusiasm in Britain for joining in any such scheme.

There was, in fact, a profound difference in outlook and psychology on the two sides of the Channel. In her finest hour Britain had stood alone. She was undefeated, she escaped occupation, she had not known bitter internal cleavages, she had no feelings of guilt, but came through with greater self-confidence, greater pride in her national virtues and national institutions than she had known for years. The Continent on the other hand had just passed through the worst ordeal of its history. Almost every family had experienced the evils of nationalism run riot, almost every country had been subjected first to national defeat and then to enemy occupation. Their national self-confidence, their national institutions had been shattered. Starting from the ruins it was imperative to develop new conceptions and more grandiose ideas that would make any future civil war between European brother nations impossible. In continental Europe a federal surrender of sovereignty thus seemed more feasible than in many less disillusioned parts of the globe.

Common opposition to the Hitler regime had brought resistance fighters and exile Governments of different nationalities closer together: over against Hitler's New Order for a united Europe under Nazi domination, the men from the *maquis* and the underground movements set an alternative ideal. As the European Resistance Movements had already declared as far back as July 1944: 'Federal Union alone can ensure the preservation of liberty and civilization on the continent of Europe, bring about economic recovery and enable the German people to play a peaceful role in European affairs.' (See also Document 1, p. 29.) For, if common fear of a third wave of German aggression seemed a bond that could unite many nations for some time, the more far-sighted also knew that it would be impossible to discriminate against Germany forever. Any such attempt would fail and breed just what it was designed to prevent. If German policy were to be subjected to international controls, and if Germany were to be an equal member in the European family of nations, then there was only one way out of the dilemma—other nations must abdicate to supranational bodies the same measure of sovereignty which they intended Germany never to regain.

Indeed the memories of the last enemy soon became less real than the fear of a new aggressor. Armed Soviet communism had advanced to the Elbe and beyond, and French and Italian communism was showing its strength in parliamentary and in direct action as far as the Channel and the Pyrenees. The year 1948 saw the communist *coup* in Prague and the beginning of the Berlin blockade. In the face of this immediate common threat of terrifying proportions, national differences loomed less large, and the unstable politics of certain countries could be buttressed by being contained in a broader-based framework. Only common defence, a common front in foreign policy and political solidarity at home seemed capable of allowing free Europe to survive the new pressures applied to it from within as well as from without.

To support the common defence effort, and to ward off the threat of subversion from within, it was moreover essential to reconstruct the devastated economies of Europe as quickly and as efficiently as possible, and only common efforts could make the best use of the scant resources available. When the American Secretary of State, George Marshall, offered Europe vast economic aid for a joint recovery programme he was facing the economic side of this challenge. The North Atlantic Treaty of 1949 (setting up NATO) institutionalized a strategic integration which was to become so close-knit with the years that important decisions in this vital field can less and less be taken or implemented by any national government alone. The economic and the military spheres were thereafter to be the two in which joint action was regarded as essential by all the West European countries. But in the eyes of many people, such action itself entailed joint political institutions; without such institutions, it was argued, democratically elected parliaments and governments were surrendering their powers and duties only to irresponsible technocrats beyond the electorate's control.

Open Differences and Latent Ambivalence

Here then the 'functionalists', most strongly represented by the British and Scandinavian governments, parted company with the federalists, who were well represented in the Governments of France, Italy and the Low Countries. It was the hallmark of the federalist that he sought joint action not least as a means for obtaining more effective common political institutions, whereas the functionalist attempted to set up such a minimum of political institutions as might be indispensable to direct the joint action that was most urgently required. While the federalist may be accused of concentrating excessively on legal formalities, the functionalist may have underrated the handicap imposed on effective everyday co-operation by the survival of national vetoes. Federalists and functionalists in the late forties failed fully to understand each other and the federalists —not by accident, but for good historical reasons—were able at the time to sway the policy of six and only six of the countries of Western Europe.

The conflict between federalists and functionalists was thus

4

to mark the whole history of post-war Europe. But there were divergencies even within the federalist camp. The United States' insistence on European co-operation had been one of the conditions of Marshall Aid. The United States was welcomed as an ally by most of those who sought to unite Europe; yet they were far from united on the policy which Europe was to pursue towards the United States once it had been united. The desire for European unity as such was thus in fact neutral between two sets of co-relative political and economic concepts.

Political unity was advocated as tending to enhance European freedom of movement—whether towards a more equal partnership within a strong Atlantic alliance or whether towards a more independent position in the world as a third force. Whichever way that decision might go, only unity, it was argued, could make it effective.

There was a parallel ambivalence or mixture of economic aims. Economic unity with its advantages of larger markets and greater specialization of production was advocated as a means of redressing the balance of dollar payments. But for some the first objective was to form a regional bloc embracing only Europe and the countries associated with it overseas, while others saw the discriminatory removal of economic barriers (between the countries of Europe but not against the rest of the world) as a tactical move to strengthen the economies of Europe for full convertibility and non-discriminatory trading relationships with the whole world.

'Third Force' and regionalist concepts in particular were linked closely with a further concern. The rise of the countries of Asia and Africa to a new influence and a new power in world affairs occupied much of federalist thought. Their idealization of European tradition forced many European federalists to take a gloomy view of this imminent shift in the constellation of world power. European political unity would not stem the tide. But some (particularly French circles) hoped it would at least buttress the 'civilizing presence' of Europe overseas, while others, faced with the same situation at one remove, felt unity was desperately needed to rehabilitate Europe morally in the eyes of world opinion and to mark the abandonment of the national concept by the very nations that had served as the model for nationalism overseas. Given the rate of expansion of the Afro-Asian countries, economic unity might not keep European resources ahead of the resources available to Afro-Asian countries for very long, but it might produce a margin of economic manoeuvre that would allow Europe to provide more aid to those countries and thereby cushion and guide even as it accelerated their progress to positions of world power.

The European movement also cut across domestic political fronts. Economic unity was advocated by free trade liberals who wished to diminish the impact of political boundaries and the influence of national governments on economic life. Yet among its foremost champions there were also those who regarded the national economy as too small an entity for effective planning, and who strove to set up supranational authorities to direct production and trade on a vaster international scale. In the field of industry, the European Communities broadly subscribe to a system of full competition; in the fields of atomic energy and agriculture, on the other hand, planning and the more restrictive agricultural interests seem to have triumphed.

Even the historic cleavage of clericals and anti-clericals was bridged by the European idea. Certainly three of the men in the van of the movement were devout Catholics born in Lothair's Middle Kingdom, an area where the liberal conception of the world and its denizens as naturally divisible into neat nation-states appears unsophisticated in the extreme: Robert Schuman, a German during the First World War, Prime Minister of France: Alcide de Gasperi, a Deputy in the Vienna Diet while Austria-Hungary was at war with Italy, Prime Minister of Italy; and Konrad Adenauer, the non-combatant anti-Prussian mayor of Cologne who flirted with the idea of separating the Rhineland from Prussia after the First World War. To them the restoration of Charlemagne's empire of a thousand years before, with the cultural unity it implied, had an emotional appeal. But the stalwarts of the movement came also from the ranks of the anti-clerical left, organized, in the early post-war years, in the Socialist Movement for a United States of Europe. The Socialist Paul-Henri Spaak, a former Belgian Prime Minister, provided the personal driving force in the drafting of the Rome Treaties, and the French Socialist leader Guy Mollet was Prime Minister during the

6

critical phases of the Common Market negotiations and secured the votes of 100 out of the 101 French Socialist deputies in favour of their ratification.

The European idea was thus originally neutral in foreign policy between a third force concept and the Atlantic alliance, undecided in trade policy between regionalism and multilateralism, ambivalent in its attitude to the problems of emergent nations in Africa and Asia, silent in cultural and educational matters between Catholicism and anti-clericalism, and neutral also in economic policy between *laisser-faire* liberalism and socialist planning. Approached from very diverse points of view European unity seemed to make sense to continental leaders, to small but highly articulate pressure groups, and to many of the war and post-war generation: it would give greater scope to Europe for whatever policy aims were envisaged. On some of these issues Britain could have turned the scales between rival concepts—if only she had not stood aloof. A sudden realization of continental federation could have produced sharp conflicts between federalists over the use to which unity was to be put; as it was, the long common struggle and the course of post-war events (with socialism and capitalism opting for the security of marriage) softened the contrasts of ultimate aim and produced not merely international but also inter-party understanding. Only the communists in every parliament of the Six consistently voted against integration.

The Birth of 'The Six'

The year of Prague and of the Berlin blockade saw two beginnings made in the organization of Western Europe: the Convention for European Economic Co-operation, signed in April, 1948, and the Hague Congress in the following month. The first set up the Organization for European Economic Co-operation (OEEC) as a functional, inter-governmental body to assure the distribution of Marshall Aid funds, to co-ordinate investment programmes, and to see that trade started moving again between the countries of Western Europe. The Hague Congress, on the other hand, was the first big demonstration by the federalists and their sympathizers. Men

7

like Churchill, Ramadier and Adenauer, Reynaud, van Zeeland and Hallstein called for the economic and political integration of Western Europe and for a deliberative assembly of European parliamentarians. As a result of their pressure, they obtained the first official political institution of a united Europe: the Council of Europe, inaugurated in Strasbourg in 1949.

The Council of Europe consists of two political organs: a Committee of Ministers (usually the Foreign Ministers of the Member States) most of whose major decisions require a unanimous vote; and a Consultative Assembly of Representatives (almost always national members of Parliament) appointed by the Parliament or Government of each country, free to harmonize views and frame recommendations on all but defence matters, but without any legislative power and without any executive responsible to it. This Assembly did however serve as the great forum in which the future shape of a united Europe was debated, in which Churchill, Macmillan, Sandys, Kilmuir, Morrison, Dalton and other leading British parliamentarians could meet with other European politicians and in which, above all, the champions of European unity could formulate their next tactical aims and exercise pressure to translate them into reality.

Impatient of the purely consultative role of their Assembly, these Europeans called for a supranational authority with limited functions but real powers. Throughout 1949 and above all 1950, the Consultative Assembly pressed for the revision of its own Statute in order to allow at least a minimal federal authority to be set up in Europe. They failed largely because of the attitude of the United Kingdom. Britain, under the Labour Government, was concerned about the loss of economic sovereignty and the right to plan its economy in a Europe which might be predominantly non-socialist. Many continental federalists were deceived by Churchill's oratory and bitterly disappointed when, after he became Prime Minister again in 1951, Britain would make no further move. Whether under the Labour or the Conservative Government, links with the Commonwealth were regarded as precluding too close links with the countries of Europe. The traditions of British foreign policy—to hold the balance but never to become entirely involved in Europe—as well as the empirical approach which

8

was thought incompatible with rigid constitution-making, were all invoked against British participation in a European federation, whatever the limits of its competence. The British counter-proposal was always for functional co-operation, and where Britain refused to go, the countries of Scandinavia would not go either.

The great divide came in the summer of 1950, when Robert Schuman, the French Minister for Foreign Affairs, proposed 'as a first step in the federation of Europe', to 'make it plain that any war between France and Germany becomes, not merely unthinkable but materially impossible', that 'the whole of Franco-German coal and steel production be placed under a common higher authority' open to other European countries. (See Document 3, p. 37.) It is not to impugn the purity of French motives to say that they were mixed: that, like the whole notion of a European federation itself, the Schuman Plan arose out of a concern over Germany's revival and over economic prosperity no less than over foreign policy at large.

In the early post-war years France had done what she could to control and limit German industrial activity in order to prevent her political resurgence in Europe. By 1950 the Americans had clearly decided against this policy, and Schuman's plan represented a startling but really quite logical *volte-face*. If the days of the discriminatory Ruhr Authority through which the Occupying Powers exercised their control looked like being numbered, a new egalitarian Community could perhaps achieve the same object on a permanent because non-discriminatory basis. That way, far from being looked at askance by the Americans for impeding Europe's economic recovery, France would prove the champion of political union. And in giving political expression to the unity of the Pas de Calais—Saar—Ruhr industrial complex 'always prescribed by geography, always prevented by history', the problems caused by a likely over-production of French steel and by the uncertainties in the supply of Ruhr coke to French industry might be brought nearer a solution. Moreover there was the Franco-German dispute over the Saar, then a unit politically separated from Germany and economically added to France. This was in essence a conflict over coal and steel resources: and by pooling these in any case, the Coal and Steel Community would

9

facilitate a settlement of this difficulty for Franco-German relations.

Britain, when invited to join the negotiations, refused. It was Mr. Macmillan who said at the time: 'One thing is certain, and we may as well face it. Our people will not hand over to any supranational Authority the right to close down our pits or our steelworks.' Once again, more intensive progress could be made only on a less extensive front. And so, for the first time, six nations—the Six—met round a conference table: France, Italy, the Federal Republic of Western Germany, Belgium, the Netherlands, and Luxembourg. The Treaty was signed in 1951, it came into force in 1952, and the common markets in coal, iron ore, scrap and most steels were set up in early 1953. The preamble to the Treaty made it crystal clear that coal and steel marked but a beginning, made in a chosen key sector. Other sectors were already being considered in intergovernmental discussions and in the Council of Europe: the Pflimlin plan for agriculture, a European transport community, and so forth. The aim of the Six was a full European Economic Community, set up to advance political objectives. The six Governments,

'Considering that world peace may be safeguarded only by creative efforts equal to the dangers which menace it;

Convinced that the contribution which an organized and vital Europe can bring to civilization is indispensable to the maintenance of peaceful relations:

Conscious of the fact that Europe can be built only by concrete actions which create a real solidarity and by the establishment of common bases for economic development;

Desirous of assisting through the expansion of their basic production in raising the standard of living and in furthering the works of peace:

Resolved to substitute for historic rivalries a fusion of their essential interests; to establish, by creating an economic community, the foundation of a broad and independent community among peoples long divided by bloody conflicts; and to lay the bases of institutions capable of giving direction to their future common destiny; have decided to create a European coal and steel community.'

The institutions for which the Treaty laid the basis were four: a High Authority of nine members independent of any

Government and acting in the interests of the Community as a whole; a Common Assembly, modelled on the Council of Europe's Common Assembly, which, by a two-thirds vote of censure, could force the High Authority to resign; a Council of Ministers representing the Member States; and a Court of Justice to ensure the rule of law in the integration of the Treaty. We shall meet this basic institutional pattern again in the subsequent Communities. (Compare the Chart on p. 73, Document 9.)

1950–1958: THE SUPRANATIONAL TRIPTYCH

The development towards a 'Little European' Economic Community thus begun in May 1950 was lifted sharply out of its natural course by world events and United States pressure. When war broke out in Korea, the United States demanded twelve German divisions for the defence of the European front. The French refused to consent to the re-establishment of a *Wehrmacht* and German membership in NATO. The Germans, if they were to be rearmed, demanded equality of rights. There was but one way of reconciling these three demands: a European army to which each state would contribute its European forces, all equally under joint European control. This conclusion was embodied in the draft treaty for a European Defence Community (See Document 4, p. 40)—and the European movement began a struggle that was to cost it four precious years.

Perhaps there was no alternative once the need for German rearmament was admitted. Certainly the Defence Community was seductive in federalist eyes. It demolished one of the most conspicuous and dangerous elements of national sovereignty: the absolute supremacy over armed military force. Like the European Coal and Steel Community, the European Defence Community was designed as a supranational agency with limited functions but with very real powers; also like ECSC, it was designed as a component to be built into a federal framework; more even than ECSC it cried aloud for new European institutions—and indeed it provided for an Assembly directly elected by universal suffrage to wield democratic political control.

In addition to the control evisaged in the EDC treaty itself, more far-reaching political plans were mapped out in detail before the EDC came up for ratification. Within six months of being given the task, an *ad hoc* Assembly (largely identical in membership with the Common Assembly of the Coal and Steel Community) drafted the constitution of a European Political Community based on an indissoluble union of states. (See Document 5, p. 53.) A directly elected European People's Chamber and a Senate indirectly elected by the national Parliaments were between them to form the European Parliament to which the President of the European Executive Council and his Cabinet colleagues were to be directly responsible. Both the Coal and Steel and the Defence Communities were to be integrated into this structure: the Peoples' Chamber would control the High Authority of the ECSC and the Commission of the EDC, with a single Council of Ministers and a single Court of Justice acting for all three Communities. From this political structure an Economic Community was to be derived.

The French Assembly was cautious about its approach to the ratification of EDC. Party spokesmen formulated certain conditions without the fulfilment of which, they insisted, Germany could not regain her sovereignty or be rearmed. Two of these were effective political control of the army and a solution of the Saar problem. The *ad hoc* Assembly had with its draft Constitution showed the way to the achievement of the one condition, and the plan of the Council of Europe spelled out a 'Europeanization' of the Saar. In addition, the French demanded assurances that there would always be sufficient British and United States troops in Europe to calm their fears of German rearmament. France demanded formal legal guarantees of a kind that do not come easily to Anglo-Saxon diplomacy; and although Churchill had, when in opposition, called for a European army in which 'we all should bear an honourable part', Britain refused even to give guarantees until it was too late. But this time, at any rate, the blame for the failure of a European scheme could no longer be laid exclusively at Britain's door.

Amid internal dissension of a kind hardly seen since the Dreyfus affair, the country that had originated the project prevented its realization. The final debate opened on Saturday, 28

August, continued throughout Sunday afternoon and evening, and was cut short on Monday evening by the procedure of moving the *question préalable* (analogous to our 'previous question') which was seconded by the 83-year-old Radical Edouard Herriot, speaking from his seat into a specially installed microphone (Document 6, p. 61 is only a pale reflection of the tension of that final debate). That night a coalition of the Communist Left with the Gaullist Right refused to continue the debate before either the author or the signatory to the Treaty had been given an opportunity of defending it, and got a majority of 319 to 264 votes since both Socialists and Radicals were fairly evenly split on the issue and only the Christian Democratic MRP, M. Schuman's party, was almost solidly in favour of the Treaty. What had seemed feasible and indeed almost unavoidable in 1950, when UN forces were on the retreat southwards in Korea and in France the MRP and the Socialists were in power, had now become unacceptable to the Assembly in the atmosphere of relaxing international tension after Stalin's death, with both MRP and Socialists in opposition, and the Mendes France Government refusing to commit itself on the issue.

Four arguments above all killed the EDC: it would resurrect the German army; it would destroy the army of France; it would affect French political sovereignty; and it would imply an Economic Community for which the French economy felt unprepared.

The arguments used against the EDC on the grounds that it meant the rearmament of Germany were shown up as perverse within a matter of weeks: for already on 23 October 1954, a *solution de rechange*, a second-best alternative was agreed between the Six, Britain and the United States. This was the outcome of bitter negotiations in London at the end of September and in Paris in October, trying to pick up the pieces after the defeat of EDC: and, as Dr. Adenauer put it, grotesquely enough the defeat of EDC resulted in the creation of a new German national army (see Document 7, p. 66). The Paris Treaties enlarged the Brussels Pact of 1948, which had been designed to safeguard the participants against any new German aggression by making Germany and Italy the sixth and seventh members of the organization (now re-christened Western European

Union), which thus associated Britain with the other five in the control of German rearmament. These Paris Treaties also made Western Germany into a sovereign power, gave her a national army and made her a member of NATO—the last two the very things which the EDC, to spare French feelings, had been so carefully designed to avoid. But thereafter for several years at least the movement towards the unity of Europe was freed from the defence issue, and was able—and forced—to return to the task which in 1950 it had just set itself to begin.

When the Six met again at Messina in June 1955 they decided that the next attack could not be too directly political. In effect, if not in form, the draft Political Community had been rejected with the EDC. 'The next phase in the building of a United Europe', as the Messina Resolution stated, 'must lie in the economic field'. (See Document 8, p. 69.) It was to the Economic Community foreshadowed in the ECSC treaty that the Six thus returned. Once and for all the economic arguments of French business against any form of political unity had to be cleared out of the way. Explicit safeguards and particular consideration had to be given to the special difficulties that were very real to France. Here was the indispensable tactical move without which there could be no further progress towards political integration.

The 'Overall' Economic Approach

At the same time there were new and important economic reasons for proceeding towards a Common Market in Europe.

For lack of gold and dollars, when raw materials, machinery, and goods of all kinds were in heavy demand, all the countries of Europe had maintained or imposed strict import controls immediately after the war. Trade between them was on the basis of a bilateral bartering of goods for goods, with very little credit granted to allow for temporary disparities between import and export values. In order to overcome the restriction and distortion of trade which this system entailed, the Organization for European Economic Co-operation in 1949 launched its programme of trade liberalization: the member countries pledged themselves to abolish quantitative restrictions on a certain percentage of imports from each other, and this 'liberalization percentage' was progressively raised. Trade could thus expand and become multilateral on a regional basis.

But to expand and multilateralize trade it was necessary to expand and multilateralize payments. In 1950, therefore, OEEC set up its European Payments Union. This system allowed multilateralized payments by arranging for all intra-European payments regardless of origin or destination to be settled not by individual countries with each other, but by a monthly net settlement by each country with the European Payments Union itself. This institution also provided certain very important automatic credit facilities.

Six years after OEEC took up its work, intra-European trade had more than doubled in volume. But further progress was proving slow. The intergovernmental structure of OEEC was too loose for its recommendations to be compelling. France, for example, was falling badly short of her liberalization commitments and was counteracting liberalization by imposing a special levy on imports. Other countries also were not fulfilling their obligations, and they, too, pleaded special difficulties as an explanation as to why they could not keep pace. Denmark, Greece, Turkey and Iceland complained that, while they were attempting to reduce quantitative restrictions on the imports of industrial products, the industrial countries were not reducing their restrictions on the import of agricultural produce and foodstuffs to a corresponding extent. Indeed, in consideration of the special political, social, and economic difficulties caused by shifts of production from agriculture to industry, the liberalization system allowed the industrial countries to maintain higher restrictions on agricultural imports than the agricultural countries were allowed to maintain on industrial goods. Thirdly, the group of Benelux and Scandinavian low-tariff countries complained that, when they liberalized the import of a commodity, this abolished almost all the protection for their producers and their balance of payments: when a high-tariff country liberalized imports, the customs duty still maintained a heavy discrimination against the foreign producer and reduced the impact on its balance of payments.

In spite of the formal symmetry of the liberalization system, it thus lacked an effective material reciprocity between agricultural and industrial, and between high-tariff and low-tariff countries; quantitative restrictions in many cases were maintained less to protect the balance of payments than to protect individual producers and industries; and the merely intergovernmental machinery which did not ultimately affect national independence of action still allowed a country to cut its imports from its neighbours when internal adjustments would have seemed preferable from a European point of view.

Where the obvious problem of tariffs was concerned, there were political and historical reasons why OEEC had never made any more. In 1948 to secure imports at all had mattered far more than their price. Quotas could be mutually abolished by swift executive action, while tariff reductions would have involved the agreement of eighteen legislatures. The reduction of tariffs was being investigated on a world basis under the General Agreement on Tariffs and Trade (GATT) that had been concluded in 1947 between originally 23 countries stretching from Brazil to Burma. Furthermore it was a principle of GATT that tariffs were not to be lowered on a discriminatory basis. Plainly, Europe had no desire unilaterally to lower her tariffs against the rest of the world at this time; therefore intra-European tariffs could not be lowered either.

By 1955 at least four of the six countries were afraid that OEEC's attempts to liberalize trade within Europe were yielding diminishing returns. The Benelux countries had already formed a customs union of their own and were impatient with the slow rate of progress of their neighbours. Holland in particular, simultaneously an agricultural and a low-tariff country, was anxious to see further advance. Within OEEC the low-tariff countries requested that the problem of trade barriers be treated as a whole, but little concrete action could then be expected on the level of the eighteen states that made up OEEC.

The provisions of GATT did, however, provide a way out. Under Article XXIV tariffs could be reduced on a regional basis provided they were reduced to zero over a reasonable period of time. It was under this Article that Benelux had been formed. This Article could now be used to solve at the same time the political problem posed by the failure of EDC and the economic problem posed by the slowing down of OEEC progress. Thus at the conference of Messina in 1955, on the proposal of the Netherlands delegation, the economic and the political streams of thought merged once more. The European movement returned to that economic path towards political unity chosen in 1950, which the failure of the Defence Community had shown to be of vital significance, and which was also thrust into the foreground by the impasse within OEEC.

The Rome Treaties

At the Conference of Messina in June 1955, the Foreign Ministers of the Six set up an inter-governmental committee of experts under the chairmanship of M. Spaak, then Belgian Foreign Minister, which met in Brussels for nine months to explore ways and means of pooling Europe's resources for the development of nuclear energy and of setting up a Common Market and customs union. The Committee's report, presented in April 1956, prepared the way for the political negotiations (see Document 8, p. 69).

The Treaties themselves were drafted in some haste to exploit the political constellation of 1955–7, when M. Mollet was French Prime Minister, before Dr. Adenauer had to face his electorate in the autumn of 1957, and while the economies of Europe were experiencing a boom. The negotiations were an intricate mixture of academic exercises in abstruse economic theory and poker games of political skill. To the pure economist without knowledge of the course of the negotiations the provisions of the Treaty may thus sometimes seem strange. But as its aims are political, so its methods are politically conditioned. Though radical in effect, the transformation will be gradual and gather momentum with time. In three stages to be completed within twelve years, the political institutions are to merge the five component national markets into a single Common Market; and in the minds of the draftsmen of the Treaty, their economic task is chiefly valued as a step towards political integration—in the words of the preamble 'an ever closer union'.

The economic system envisaged is summarized in the second and third articles of the EEC Treaty:

'Article 2:

It shall be the aim of the Community by establishing a Common Market and progressively approximating the economic policies of Member States, to promote throughout the Community a harmonious development of economic activities, a continuous and balanced expansion, an increased stability, an accelerated rise in standards of living and closer relations between its Member States.

Article 3:

For the purposes set out in the preceding Article, the activities of the Community shall include, under the conditions and with the timing provided for in this Treaty:

(*a*) the elimination, as between Member States, of customs duties and of quantitative restrictions in regard to the importation and exportation of goods, as well as of all other measures with equivalent effect;

(*b*) the establishment of a common customs tariff and a common commercial policy towards third countries;

(*c*) the abolition, as between Member States, of the obstacles to the free movement of persons, services and capital;

(*d*) the inauguration of a common agricultural policy;

(*e*) the inauguration of a common transport policy;

(*f*) the establishment of a system ensuring that competition shall not be distorted in the Common Market;

(*g*) the application of procedures which shall make it possible to co-ordinate the economic policies of Member States and to remedy disequilibria in their balances of payments;

(*h*) the approximation of their respective legislations to the extent necessary for the functioning of the Common Market;

(*i*) the creation of a European Social Fund in order to improve the employment opportunities of workers and to contribute to the raising of their standard of living;

(*j*) the establishment of a European Investment Bank intended to facilitate the economic expansion of the Community through the creation of new resources; and

(*k*) the association of overseas countries and territories with the Community with a view to increasing trade and to pursuing jointly their effort towards economic and social development.'

Such a system is neither one of centralized public planning, nor one of *laisser-faire* competition. It is neither one of nationalization nor one of purely private enterprise. It is the agreed upshot of a much more adaptable, undogmatic approach along different paths to the different problems presented by the economies of the Six in the last half of the twentieth century. For atomic energy the Euratom Treaty contains strong elements of public ownership and public control. For agriculture the EEC system is one of state support and quality control. For underdeveloped regions it is one of public finance and public encouragement of private capital. For transport it is one involving central plans and a mixture of European, national and private enterprise. It provides a harmonized monetary framework and, for most of industry, a system of harmonized rules within which each firm is free to compete: whether it be a private firm like Fiat, a nationalized firm like Renault, or a de-nationalized one like Volkswagen. The system neither encourages nor prevents nationalization or de-nationalization. Apart from the tariff reductions, most of the real decisions are to be taken by the institutions of the Community on the proposal of a supranational Commission by the Council of Ministers at first by unanimity, but later by qualified majority vote.

It was this pragmatic, un-ideological approach that allowed agreement to be reached and all the drafting to be completed less than a year after the intergovernmental negotiations proper started. On 24 March 1957, the two Rome Treaties, that establishing the European Economic Community and that setting up the European Atomic Energy Community (Euratom) were signed on the Capitoline Hill in Rome. They were ratified by overwhelming majorities of Socialists and Liberals no less than Christian Democrats in all the member states within a few months, and entered into force on 1 January 1958.

1958–1966: THE CHANGE OF REPUBLIC IN FRANCE

The year 1958 was taken up in Brussels by the installation of the Commission and its services, preparations for the first tariff cuts on 1 January 1959, and preliminary work on common policies in that whole gamut of questions in which the Community is to act. But the most important event by far for the

Community's future that year did not happen in Brussels, or even in Europe, but in Algeria: and on 13 May as a result of events in Algeria, the Fourth Republic in effect ceased to exist when General de Gaulle returned from his retirement at Colombey-les-deux-Eglises to become head of the government. The Fourth Republic, it should be said, would have been by far the most successful regime France has had since Napoleon, had it not failed: the French economic miracle performed behind the kaleidoscopically changing Prime Ministers by the French permanent civil service and a new generation of technically-minded businessmen was no less miraculous—in some ways rather more so—than the German or the Italian. But the inability to solve the problem of decolonization of an African country with a large white settler population brought down the Fourth Republic almost extraneously just at the moment when the ordinary consuming public was about at last to taste the rewards of twelve years of austerity and inflation for heavy industrial investment, hardships which had done much to deprive the Fourth Republic of popular support.

The first effects of the policies of the Fifth Republic, which thus reaped the harvest of all the sacrifices imposed by the Fourth, were by no means injurious to the nascent Common Market. President de Gaulle's new programme at the end of 1958 was one of *verité et sévérité*: a frankness which recognized the creeping depreciation of the franc by a devaluation of 17 per cent, and a discipline that prevented the advantages of this devaluation being frittered away in a new bout of inflation. The new President was prepared to abide by the country's international treaty obligations, and thanks to the new relative price relationships between French industry and that of her partners no escape clauses had to be invoked. Indeed once the currency adjustment had been made, the basic health of the French economy stood revealed: and French business, much to its own surprise, soon found its wings in the new air of competition and expansion across national boundaries. France's exports to her EEC partners doubled in three years and her overall deficit turned into a handsome surplus that allowed her to accumulate a tidy foreign exchange reserve (see Document 9, Tables C and D, pp. 77, 78 and 81).

If the new French Government thus felt at peace with the

economic aspects of the EEC, only insisting all the time that
the common market for industrial goods must in fairness be
matched as soon as possible by a common agricultural market,
there were, however, two other aspects on which the French
President soon took issue with his partners, on which he has
indeed not yet reached a settlement with them, and on which
it is unlikely that he ever really will. The first of these issues is
the political organization of the Community and the range of
matters to be dealt with on a Community basis; the second is the
question of the Community's relations with the rest of the world.

The Issue of Institutional Development

While President de Gaulle could accept the economic benefits
of mutual reductions in industrial tariffs (which by 1966 had
reduced the pre-existing customs duties between the Six by
four-fifths), he was caught in something of a dilemma where
agricultural policy was concerned: for here any automatic
elimination of tariffs was useless, and what was required was a
positive common policy on farm prices, farm imports, and
public measures to raise farm productivity. Negative measures
like the elimination of tariffs could be taken through the treaty
automatism: but though a common agricultural policy was
required by the Treaty, it was not spelt out in the Treaty
itself, but needed the full play of the Community institutions to
work it out and agree on it between all six partner states.
Repeatedly therefore the French negotiators made the progress
(and the acceleration) of the automatic industrial tariff
disarmament within the EEC dependent on agreements, if not
on actual agricultural policies then at least on deadlines by
which those agricultural policies must be agreed and implemented. So that progressively as industrial pressures
combined with political ambitions to complete the industrial
customs union ahead of schedule (and if possible by mid-1967),
the time-table for a common farm policy was also brought
forward.

When in January 1962 the Six agreed to pass from the first
to the second stage of the Treaty's implementation, it followed
that as from 1 January 1966 with the beginning of the third
stage (which begins automatically unless all six countries agree

to hold it up) a wide variety of questions, including those of foreign trade and some of agriculture, could be settled by a qualified majority of member states, the national veto being abolished from that date. France was extremely anxious that as much as possible of farm policy should be settled before then, for it was her farmers who had most to gain from free access to the markets of the other five at a guaranteed price that was low enough to put in particular many of the German farmers out of business.

The EEC Commission, trading on this French eagerness, put forward in spring and summer of 1965 proposals that were indeed very advantageous to French farming, but which would also have given the Commission a huge income from levies on imports of agricultural produce into the Community—a direct income independent of the annual votes provided by the national governments. The French jibbed at this package deal, claimed that the Commission in introducing these budgetary measures into the farm settlement had exceeded its powers, and that unless the other five yielded, France's agreement to pass on to the second stage in 1962 must be regarded as now being null and void for lack of that agreement on agriculture which was presupposed in French agreement at the time. Just after midnight on 30 June 1965 the French Chairman adjourned the Council meeting and for the rest of the year the French boycotted the Community's intergovernmental institutions. In his press conference of 9 September 1965, indeed, President de Gaulle brought out very clearly that it was not so much agriculture that was at stake as the whole constitutional system of majority voting after 1 January 1966, and equally the independent role and right of initiative of the Commission (see Document 14, p. 123). The compromise formula of 29 January 1966 (see Document 15, p. 128) marked a technical retreat from France's demands which showed just how costly it would be for her in economic terms to withdraw from the Community, but it also left the question of majority voting in suspense and weakened the case of the Five to the extent that it officially recognized a divergence of view: to that extent the ultimate deterrent of outvoting a country on some issue on which it refuses to compromise will have lost some of its credibility.

If France was thus in 1965–6 back-pedalling on her Treaty obligations of 1957, there had also on the other hand in the meantime been various initiatives either to intensify or to extend common institutions. The European stalwarts of the 1940s and 50s were calling above all for two types of development. Firstly they pressed for the direct election of the European Assembly as called for in the Rome Treaty itself (see Document 11, p. 104) and a consequent increase in its powers over the Community budget, a say in the appointment of the Commission, and a legislative initiative of its own. Secondly they urged the merger of the three executives and indeed of the three Communities as a whole. The first demand has been consistently opposed by the French, and not always particularly championed by the other five Governments. But on the second demand agreement was reached and a new Treaty was signed in April 1965 for the merger at least of the Executives (see Document 13, p. 119). Oddly enough this Treaty is now one of the factors in the stalemate between France and the other five, with France strongly in favour of an early merger, obviously anxious to use this opportunity in order to clip the wings of the Commission and to remove some of its most dynamic personalities, notably Dr. Hallstein and Mr. Mansholt, from the Brussels scene.

More interesting in many ways have been the efforts not so much to deepen the political structure of the three existing Communities, as to go forward towards common action outside the spheres of coal and steel, nuclear energy, and general economics—particularly into the fields of foreign policy and even defence. Such co-operation was, needless to say, envisaged on all sides as less close than the integration in economics: none of the Governments have yet seriously proposed a return to the conception of a Political Community of the 1953–4 type. The new phrase has been—paradoxically enough—a 'Political Union', which Union, however, is to be much looser than was the draft Political Community. President de Gaulle envisaged it as a concert of governments, rather than a union of peoples: it might be sanctioned by a referendum (a form of government in which he had scored some successes), but it was to remain subject to veto from any one government, and to act only if all six governments were agreed.

By 1961 the demand to relaunch Europe politically had grown strong enough for the Governments to ask their committee on the subject to submit proposals for 'giving a statutory character . . . to the union of their peoples' (see Document 12, p. 108). But the first draft submitted by M. Fouchet, its French chairman, hardly went very far, and the second draft (refurbished in 1962, it is said, by President de Gaulle personally) retreated even further, and also roused suspicions that the new Political Union would, by subordinating the existing Communities to intergovernmental institutions, deprive them of their supranational character. In the end the Committee could do little more than set out the two texts synoptically and write a commentary on the differences between them (see Document 12, p. 108).

The Community and the Outside World

At this stage however it was no longer merely the possible institutions for harmonizing foreign policy, it was also the substance of that foreign policy itself that was at stake. The problems of French relations with Africa and hence the Community's relations with Africa posed few problems: the Convention of Association annexed to the Rome Treaty was replaced after it had expired at the end of 1962, by the new Yaoundé Convention of 1963, which also opened the way for potential new Associates to negotiate a special relationship with the Community (see Document 17, p. 131). The problem lay in the Community's relations with the Anglo-Saxon world —with Britain and with the USA.

The United Kingdom had begun to watch developments on the continent with concern in 1956, when, for the first time, it began to look as if she might be excluded from a continental economic bloc and incur substantial trade discrimination. She proposed that round the customs union of the Six an industrial free trade area should be set up which would have given her the advantages of free access to the Community without any of the burdens of a common tariff, a common agricultural policy, joint policies right through the economy, or the loss of national veto rights. Negotiations for such a free trade area to include all or almost all the OEEC countries proceeded intensively until, in November 1958, M. Soustelle, at a press conference in Paris, stated categorically that the new French Government would have none of the scheme.

Seven of the other members of OEEC, led by Switzerland and Britain, then proceeded to form their own industrial free trade arrangement, the European Free Trade Association (EFTA). This has in fact succeeded in catching up on the tariff reductions between the Six, so that now industrial tariffs between Britain, Switzerland, Austria, Norway, Denmark, Sweden and Portugal are also only four-fifths of what they once were. But tariffs between the two groupings remain, and EFTA, adding only 30 million people to the United Kingdom's domestic market, is obviously a poor second best to EEC from that point of view.

So, for commercial and economic, but also and above all for political reasons, in summer 1961 Britain (and with her Norway, Denmark and Ireland) announced that she would apply under Article 237 for membership of the Economic Community. There were obviously a great many obstacles to be overcome, as Mr. Heath, the chief British negotiator, made quite clear at the outset (see Document 18, p. 151): but the British Government declared itself resolved to overcome them, and ready to take part also in the political construction of Europe.

The prospect of such an enlarged European Community—of 220 million people in one economic and also potentially political unit—could not fail to give cause for reflection in the rest of the world. President Kennedy had all along clearly urged the creation of such a unit to take its equal share with the United States as the second pillar of the Atlantic Alliance both *vis-à-vis* the Socialist and *vis-à-vis* the developing world. Indeed on it he based his whole concept of economic, military and political partnershp between an interdependent Europe and North America (see Document 19, p. 165).

But it was not to be. Not only were there strong voices raised against British entry into the Community from the right no less than the left within Britain herself (see Documents 20, 21 and 22, p. 168 onwards), leaving public opinion far from decided on the issue, not only did the negotiations over the economic difficulties drag on for fifteen months in Brussels, but

in the end a clear veto came in another press conference, on
14 January 1963, from President de Gaulle himself (see
Document 23, p. 182)—a veto directed not simply at British
conditions of entry, or at more economic competition within
the Common Market, nor even only at the threat to French
political hegemony that Britain within the Community would
imply, but directed above all at the whole concept of Atlantic
partnership, in which France feared Britain would prove to be
the 'Trojan horse' of America within the European camp.
Nothing, President de Gaulle is reported to have said privately,
proved this more than Britain's decision by the Nassau agreement of December 1962 to throw in her lot in nuclear weapons
with the United States rather than with Europe.

So the negotiations with Britain were (to put it mildly but
correctly) suspended. Britain remains a candidate for membership, but the other five declared themselves prevented from
continuing the negotiations. The fundamental difference of
approach to the place of Europe in the world however remains,
and still divides the French government from the other five
—even if there are 'Gaullist' voices to be heard in Germany and
the other countries too. It is the great remaining ambivalence
that has now broken out into open conflict: between the
Atlanticists and the Europe-for-the-Europeans. But there is
also a throw-back to sentiments of France for the French, and
hence Germany for the Germans: for the greatest danger in all
this, a danger that even Dr. Adenauer did not formulate that
night at Claridge's in 1954, is that a reawakened French
nationalism may teach and force the Germans to think in
national terms again too. This clash of philosophies is symbol-
ized and at its most acute in the question of nuclear weapons;
it plays its part in the Kennedy Round of tariff negotiations
that are the economic left-over of the frustrated concept of
Atlantic Partnership; it rumbles on in French hostility to
United States investment in French industry and has of course
found its clearest expression in France's ritual withdrawal from
NATO.

The world has of course changed, and changed radically, since
that July 1944 when clandestine meetings of the Resistance
Movements demanded a European Federal Union. Africa has

been largely decolonized, Latin America is stirring, India and Pakistan hit the headlines, China is emerging on the world scene, and Europe is only one continent among many. Franco-German war has indeed become unthinkable, but nuclear weapons complicate the issue and may make Europe inevitably secondary to the super-powers unless she aims at becoming a nuclear super-power herself, a notion that would presuppose very tight political unity indeed.

But today it is no longer from a European but from the world point of view that these European questions must be judged. The documents can guide us only as to the past. Speculation as to the future is free for all. My final assessment therefore is personal—even more so than the rest of this book. And the real interest for the student lies, not in reading this book, but in putting it down when he has finished and in applying it to a present which, at the time of writing, can only be dimly foreseen, and to a future that remains unknowable while yet on our decisions about it the fate of the planet depends.

SUGGESTED EXERCISES

Fifteen suggested exercises for students of the documents will be found at the end of the book, where the specific significance of each one of them becomes most apparent.

PART I

The Mainsprings of Supranationalism

DOCUMENT I. DRAFT DECLARATION BY THE EUROPEAN
RESISTANCE MOVEMENTS, JULY 1944

Activists from the Resistance Movements of Denmark, France,
Italy, Norway, the Netherlands, Poland, Czechoslovakia and
Yugoslavia and the Representative of an active anti-Nazi
group in Germany met in a city in Europe on 31 March, 29
April, 20 May and 6 and 7 July 1944. They drafted the following Declaration which is herewith submitted for discussion and
approval by their respective Movements and by the whole of
the Resistance Movements of Europe. They believe that they
should immediately transmit their draft to international
public opinion but reserve their right to publish it in its final
form when it has been accepted by the Movements, groups
and parties to which it is submitted.

I

Resistance to Nazi oppression, which unites the people of
Europe in the same battle, has created among them a solidarity
and a community of aim and of interest whose significance and
meaning is expressed in the fact that delegates from the
Resistance Movements of Europe have met to set out this
Declaration in which they wish to express their hopes and their
intentions for the fate of civilization and of peace.

The free men who take part today in resistance movements
are aware that the incessant fight which they are conducting
in spite of all terror on the front of internal resistance against
the war machine of the enemy is an important positive contribution to the battle being fought by the united nations and
that it gives their countries the right to take part in the building

29

of peace and of the reconstruction of Europe on the same basis as the other victorious powers.

Subscribing to the central declarations of the Atlantic Charter, they reaffirm that the life of the peoples which they represent must be based on the respect of the human individual, on security, on social justice, on the complete utilization of economic resources for the benefit of the whole and on the autonomous development of national life.

II

These aims cannot be fulfilled unless the different countries of the world agree to go beyond the dogma of the absolute sovereignty of the state and unite in a single federal organization.

The lack of unity and cohesion that still exists between the different parts of the world will not allow us to achieve immediately an organization that unites all civilizations under a single federal government. At the end of this war one will therefore have to be content with setting up a universal organization of a less ambitious kind, but one able to develop in the direction of federal unity, in which the great civilizations on which it rests will pursue the task of ensuring collective security. But this cannot be an efficient instrument of peace unless the great civilizations are organized in such a fashion that the spirit of peace and of understanding can prevail.

That is why within the framework of this universal organization the European problem must be given a more direct and a more radical solution.

III

The peace of Europe is the cornerstone of world peace. Within a single generation Europe has now been the focal centre of two world conflicts which were due above all to the existence on this continent of thirty sovereign states. This anarchy must be remedied by the creation of a Federal Union between the European peoples.

Only a Federal Union will allow the German people to participate in the life of Europe without being a danger for the rest.

Only a Federal Union will allow the problems of frontier

demarcation in areas of mixed population to be resolved—problems which will thus cease to be the object of stupid nationalist covetousness and will become simple questions of the territorial demarcation of purely administrative powers.

Only a Federal Union will allow democratic institutions to be safeguarded in such a way that countries that are insufficiently mature politically cannot endanger the general order.

Only a Federal Union will allow the economic reconstruction of the continent and the elimination of monopolies and national autarchies.

Only a Federal Union will allow a logical and natural solution to the problems of access to the sea for landlocked countries, the rational utilization of the rivers that run through more than one state, the control of straits and generally most of these problems that have upset international relations in recent years.

IV

One cannot now foresee the geographical limits of the Federal Union that will ensure the peace of Europe. But it must be sufficiently strong and sufficiently large for there to be no risk of it becoming the sphere of influence of a foreign state or the instrument of a hegemonial policy by one of its members. Moreover it must from the beginning be open to all countries that belong either wholly or partly to Europe and which can and wish to become members of it. The Federal Union must be based on a declaration of civil, political and economic rights which guarantees the free development of the human personality and the normal functioning of democratic institutions; moreover it must rest on a declaration of the rights of minorities to an autonomous existence compatible with the integrity of the nation states of which they form a part.

The Federal Union must not prejudice the right of each of the member countries to solve its own special problems according to its own ethnic and cultural characteristics. But given the experiences and the failures of the League of Nations, the member states must irrevocably surrender to the Federation those aspects of their sovereignty that deal with the defence of their territory, relations with states outside the Federal Union, and international trade and communications.

The Federal Union must essentially have (i) a government responsible not to the governments of the various member states but to their peoples, over which it must be able to exercise direct jurisdiction within the limits of its powers; (ii) an army placed under the orders of this government and excluding all other national armies; (iii) a supreme tribunal which will judge all questions as to the interpretation of the federal constitution and which will settle any differences there may be between member states or between the states and the federation.

V

The peace to be born out of this war must be founded on justice and progress and not on revenge and reaction. It must show itself implacable against all war criminals, whose impunity would be an insult to the sacrifice made by the war dead and particularly the anonymous heroes of the European Resistance. Germany and its satellites must take part in the economic reconstruction of the regions they have devastated, but Germany must be helped and if necessary forced to transform her own political and economic structure so that she can take her place in the Federal Union. For that she must be totally disarmed and temporarily subjected to a federal control which shall have as its principal tasks:

To entrust power to those sincerely democratic elements that have fought an unequivocal battle against Nazism;

To reconstruct a decentralized and democratic state where there will be no trace left of Prussian bureaucracy and militarism;

To demand the radical destruction of the feudal system of agriculture and of industry;

To integrate the heavy and chemical industry of Germany into European industrial organization so that it can no longer be used for German nationalist aims;

To ensure that the education of German youth does not follow Nazi, militarist or totalitarian doctrines.

VI

The undersigned movements of resistance recognize the need for an active participation of the united nations in the solution of the European problem, but demand that all the measures that are taken between the end of hostilities and the establishment of peace are taken with a view to the needs of the federal organization.

They appeal to all the spiritual and political forces of the world and particularly to those of the united nations for help in achieving the aims set out in this Declaration.

They undertake to consider their respective national problems as special aspects of the European problem as a whole, and they decide to set up immediately a permanent office to co-ordinate their efforts for the liberation of their countries, for the organization of the Federal Union of the European peoples, and to build peace and justice in the world.

DOCUMENT 2. EXTRACT FROM MR. WINSTON CHURCHILL'S SPEECH AT THE UNIVERSITY OF ZURICH, 19 SEPTEMBER 1946.

I wish to speak to you today about the tragedy of Europe. This noble continent, comprising on the whole the fairest and the most cultivated regions of the earth, enjoying a temperate and equable climate, is the home of all the great parent races of the western world. It is the fountain of Christian faith and Christian ethics. It is the origin of most of the culture, arts, philosophy and science both of ancient and modern times. If Europe were once united in the sharing of its common inheritance, there would be no limit to the happiness, to the prosperity and glory which its three or four hundred million people would enjoy. Yet it is from Europe that have sprung that series of frightful nationalistic quarrels, originated by the Teutonic nations, which we have seen even in this twentieth century and in our own lifetime, wreck the peace and mar the prospects of all mankind.

And what is the plight to which Europe has been reduced? Some of the smaller States have indeed made a good recovery, but over wide areas a vast quivering mass of tormented, hungry, care-worn and bewildered human beings gape at the ruins of their cities and homes, and scan the dark horizons for the approach of some new peril, tyranny or terror. Among the victors there is a babel of jarring voices; among the vanquished the sullen silence of despair. That is all that Europeans, grouped in so many ancient States and nations, that is all that the Germanic Powers have got by tearing each other to pieces and spreading havoc far and wide. Indeed, but for the fact that the great Republic across the Atlantic Ocean has at length realized that the ruin or enslavement of Europe would involve their own fate as well, and has stretched out hands of succour and guidance, the Dark Ages would have returned in all their cruelty and squalor. They may still return.

Yet all the while there is a remedy which, if it were generally and spontaneously adopted, would as if by a miracle transform the whole scene, and would in a few years make all Europe, or the greater part of it, as free and as happy as Switzerland is today. What is this sovereign remedy? It is to re-create the European Family, or as much of it as we can, and provide it with a structure under which it can dwell in peace, in safety and in freedom. We must build a kind of United States of Europe. In this way only will hundreds of millions of toilers be able to regain the simple joys and hopes which make life worth living. The process is simple. All that is needed is the resolve of hundreds of millions of men and women to do right instead of wrong and gain as their reward blessing instead of cursing.

Much work has been done upon this task by the exertions of the Pan-European Union which owes so much to Count Coudenhove-Kalergi and which commanded the services of the famous French patriot and statesman, Aristide Briand. There is also that immense body of doctrine and procedure, which was brought into being amid high hopes after the First World War, as the League of Nations. The League of Nations did not fail because of its principles or conceptions. It failed because these principles were deserted by those States who had brought it into being. It failed because the Governments of those days feared to face the facts, and act while time remained. This disaster must not be repeated. There is therefore much knowledge and material with which to build; and also bitter dear-bought experience.

I was very glad to read in the newspapers two days ago

34

that my friend President Truman had expressed his interest and sympathy with this great design. There is no reason why a regional organization of Europe should in any way conflict with the world organization of the United Nations. On the contrary, I believe that the larger synthesis will only survive if it is founded upon coherent natural groupings. There is already a natural grouping in the Western Hemisphere. We British have our own Commonwealth of Nations. These do not weaken, on the contrary they strengthen, the world organization. They are in fact its main support. And why should there not be a European group which could give a sense of enlarged patriotism and common citizenship to the distracted peoples of this turbulent and mighty continent and why should it not take its rightful place with other great groupings in shaping the destinies of men? In order that this should be accomplished there must be an act of faith in which millions of families speaking many languages must consciously take part.

We all know that the two world wars through which we have passed arose out of the vain passion of a newly-united Germany to play the dominating part in the world. In this last struggle crimes and massacres have been committed for which there is no parallel since the invasions of the Mongols in the fourteenth century and no equal at any time in human history. The guilty must be punished. Germany must be deprived of the power to rearm and make another aggressive war. But when all this has been done, as it will be done, as it is being done, there must be an end to retribution. There must be what Mr. Gladstone many years ago called 'a blessed act of oblivion'. We must all turn our backs upon the horrors of the past. We must look to the future. We cannot afford to drag forward across the years that are to come the hatreds and revenges which have sprung from the injuries of the past. If Europe is to be saved from infinite misery, and indeed from final doom, there must be an act of faith in the European family and an act of oblivion against all the crimes and follies of the past.

Can the free peoples of Europe rise to the height of these resolves of the soul and instincts of the spirit of man? If they can, the wrongs and injuries which have been inflicted will have been washed away on all sides by the miseries which

D   35

have been endured. Is there any need for further floods of agony? Is it the only lesson of history that mankind is unteachable? Let there be justice, mercy and freedom. The peoples have only to will it, and all will achieve their hearts' desire.

I am now going to say something that will astonish you. The first step in the re-creation of the European family must be a partnership between France and Germany. In this way only can France recover the moral leadership of Europe. There can be no revival of Europe without a spiritually great France and a spiritually great Germany. The structure of the United States of Europe, if well and truly built, will be such as to make the material strength of a single state less important. Small nations will count as much as large ones and gain their honour by their contribution to the common cause. The ancient states and principalities of Germany, freely joined together for mutual convenience in a federal system, might each take their individual place among the United States of Europe. I shall not try to make a detailed programme for hundreds of millions of people who want to be happy and free, prosperous and safe, who wish to enjoy the four freedoms of which the great President Roosevelt spoke, and live in accordance with the principles embodied in the Atlantic Charter. If this is their wish, they have only to say so, and means can certainly be found, and machinery erected, to carry that wish into full fruition.

But I must give you a warning. Time may be short. At present there is a breathing-space. The cannon have ceased firing. The fighting has stopped; but the dangers have not stopped. If we are to form the United States of Europe or whatever name or form it may take, we must begin now.

In these present days we dwell strangely and precariously under the shield and protection of the atomic bomb. The atomic bomb is still only in the hands of a State and nation which we know will never use it except in the cause of right and freedom. But it may well be that in a few years this awful agency of destruction will be widespread and the catastrophe following from its use by several warring nations will not only bring to an end all that we call civilization, but may possibly disintegrate the globe itself.

I must now sum up the propositions which are before you.

36

Our constant aim must be to build and fortify the strength of UNO. Under and within that world concept we must re-create the European family in a regional structure called, it may be, the United States of Europe. The first step is to form a Council of Europe. If at first all the States of Europe are not willing or able to join the Union, we must nevertheless proceed to assemble and combine those who will and those who can. The salvation of the common people of every race and of every land from war or servitude must be established on solid foundations and must be guarded by the readiness of all men and women to die rather than submit to tyranny. In all this urgent work, France and Germany must take the lead together. Great Britain, the British Commonwealth of Nations, mighty America, and I trust Soviet Russia—for then indeed all would be well—must be the friends and sponsors of the new Europe and must champion its right to live and shine.

DOCUMENT 3. EXTRACT FROM M. ROBERT SCHUMAN'S DECLARATION of 9 MAY 1950

World peace cannot be safeguarded without the making of constructive efforts proportionate to the dangers which threaten it.

The contribution which an organized and living Europe can bring to civilization is indispensable to the maintenance of peaceful relations. In taking upon herself for more than twenty years the role of champion of a united Europe, France has always had as her essential aim the service of peace. A united Europe was not achieved, and we have war.

Europe will not be made all at once, or according to a single, general plan. It will be built through concrete achievements, which first create a *de facto* solidarity. The gathering of the nations of Europe requires the elimination of the age-old opposition of France and Germany. The first concern in any action undertaken must be these two countries.

With this aim in view, the French Government proposes that action be taken immediately on one limited but decisive point. The French Government proposes that the whole of Franco-German coal and steel production be placed under a common 'higher authority', within the framework of an organization open to participation by the other countries of Europe.

The pooling of coal and steel production will immediately provide for the setting-up of common bases for economic development as a first step in the federation of Europe, and will change the destinies of those regions which have long been devoted to the manufacture of munitions of war, of which they have been the most constant victims.

The solidarity in production thus established will make it plain that any war between France and Germany becomes, not merely unthinkable, but materially impossible. The setting-up of this powerful production unit, open to all countries willing to take part, and eventually capable of providing all the member countries with the basic elements of industrial production on the same terms, will lay the real foundations for their economic unification.

This production will be offered to the world as a whole without distinction or exception, with the aim of contributing to the raising of living standards and the promotion of peaceful achievements. Europe, with new means at her disposal, will be able to pursue the realization of one of her essential tasks, the development of the African continent.

In this way there will be realized, simply and speedily, that fusion of interests which is indispensable to the establishment of a common economic system; and that will be the leaven from which may grow a wider and deeper community between countries long opposed to one another by sanguinary divisions.

By pooling basic production and by setting up a new higher authority, whose decisions will be binding on France, Germany and other member countries, these proposals will build the first concrete foundation of the European Federation which is indispensable to the preservation of peace.

In order to promote the realization of the objectives it has thus defined, the French Government is ready to open negotiations on the following basis.

The task with which this common 'higher authority' will be charged will be that of securing in the shortest possible time the modernization of production and the improvement of its quality; the supply of coal and steel on identical terms to the

French and German markets, as well as to the markets of other member countries; the development in common of exports to other countries; and the equalization as well as improvement of the living conditions of the workers in these industries.

To achieve these objectives, starting from the very disparate conditions in which the productions of the member countries are at present situated, certain transitional measures will have to be instituted, such as a production and investment plan, compensating machinery for equalizing prices, and an amortization fund to facilitate the rationalization of production. The movement of coal and steel between member countries will immediately be freed of all Customs duties; it will not be permissible to apply differential transport rates to them. Conditions will gradually be created which will spontaneously ensure the most rational distribution of production at the highest level of productivity.

In contrast to international cartels, which aim at dividing up and exploiting the national markets by means of restrictive practices and the maintenance of high profits, the proposed organization will ensure the fusion of the markets and the expansion of production. . . .

The common High Authority entrusted with the working of the whole scheme will consist of independent persons chosen by the governments on a basis of equality; a president will be chosen by common agreement by the governments; its decisions will be mandatory in France, in Germany and in the other member countries. Appropriate provisions will ensure the necessary channels of appeal against the decisions of the High Authority. A representative of the United Nations accredited to this authority will be charged with making a public report twice a year to the United Nations Organization dealing with the working of the new organization, particularly with regard to the safeguarding of its peaceful objectives.

The institution of the High Authority does not in any way prejudice the system of ownership of firms. In undertaking its task, the common High Authority will take into account the powers conferred on the International Ruhr Authority and the obligations of all types imposed on Germany to the extent that these are still in force.

DOCUMENT 4. EXTRACTS FROM THE (UNRATIFIED) TREATY
ESTABLISHING A EUROPEAN DEFENCE COMMUNITY, SIGNED IN
PARIS ON 27 MAY 1952

The President of the Federal Republic of Germany, His
Majesty the King of the Belgians, the President of the French
Republic, the President of the Italian Republic, Her Royal
Highness the Grand Duchess of Luxembourg, Her Majesty the
Queen of the Netherlands,

Determined in co-operation with the free nations and in the
spirit of the Charter of the United Nations to contribute
to the maintenance of peace, more particularly by ensuring
the defence of Western Europe against any aggression in
close collaboration with organizations having the same purpose;

Considering the fullest possible integration to the extent
compatible with military necessities, of the human and
material elements of their Defence Forces assembled within a
supranational European organization to be the best means for
the attainment of this aim with the necessary speed and
efficiency;

Convinced that such integration will lead to the most rational
and economical use of their countries' resources, in particular
through the establishment of a common budget and common
armaments programmes;

Determined thereby to secure the expansion of their military
strength without detriment to social progress;

Anxious to preserve the spiritual and moral values which are
the common heritage of their peoples, and convinced that
within the common force formed without discrimination
between the Member States, national patriotism, far from being
weakened, will be consolidated and harmonized in a broader
framework;

Recognizing that this is a new and essential step towards
the creation of a united Europe;

Have resolved to set up a European Defence Community
and to this end have designated as plenipotentiaries:

The President of the Federal Republic of Germany,

Dr Konrad Adenauer, Chancellor, Minister for Foreign
Affairs;

His Majesty the King of the Belgians,
M. Paul van Zeeland, Minister for Foreign Affairs;
The President of the French Republic,
M. Robert Schuman, Minister for Foreign Affairs;
The President of the Italian Republic,
M. De Gasperi, Minister for Foreign Affairs;
Her Royal Highness the Grand Duchess of Luxembourg,
M. Bech, Minister for Foreign Affairs;
Her Majesty the Queen of the Netherlands,
M. Stikker, Minister for Foreign Affairs;
Who, after exchanging their full powers, found in good and due form, have agreed as follows:

PART I. FUNDAMENTAL PRINCIPLES

Chapter I. The European Defence Community

Article 1. The High Contracting Parties, by the present Treaty, set up among themselves a European Defence Community, supranational in character, comprising common institutions, common Armed Forces, and a common budget.

Article 2. (1) The objectives of the Community are exclusively defensive.

(2) Consequently, under the conditions set forth in this Treaty, it shall ensure the security of Member States against any aggression by taking part in Western defence within the framework of the North Atlantic Treaty; by integrating the defence forces of the Member States; and by the rational and economical employment of their resources.

(3) Any armed attack against any of the Member States in Europe or against the European Defence Forces shall be considered an armed attack on all Member States.

The Member States and the European Defence Forces shall afford to the State or forces so attacked all the military and other aid in their power.

Article 3. (1) The Community shall act in the least onerous and most efficient manner possible. It shall only take action to the extent necessary for the fulfilment of its task, and in so doing it shall respect essential public liberties and the fundamental rights of individuals. It shall be vigilant to ensure that the interests of Member States receive all the consideration compatible with its own essential interests.

(2) To enable the Community to attain its objectives, the Member States shall make available the appropriate contributions, determined according to the provisions of Articles 86 and 93 of this Treaty.

Article 4. The Community shall work in collaboration with the free nations and with any organization having the same objectives as itself.

Article 5. The Community shall work in close co-operation with the North Atlantic Treaty Organization.

Article 6. The present Treaty shall in no way discriminate between its Member States.

Article 7. The Community shall have juridical personality . . .

Article 8. (1) The institutions of the Community shall be: a Council of Ministers, hereinafter known as the Council; a Common Assembly, hereinafter known as the Assembly; a Board of Commissioners of the Community, hereinafter known as the Board of Commissioners; a Court of Justice, hereinafter known as the Court . . .

Chapter II. European Defence Forces

Article 9. The Armed Forces of the Community, hereinafter known as the 'European Defence Forces', shall be composed of units made available to the Community by its Member States, with a view to their fusion under the conditions laid down in this Treaty.

No Member State shall recruit or maintain national armed forces other than those for which provision is made in Article 10 below.

Article 10. (1) Member States may recruit and maintain national armed forces intended for employment in non-European territories for whose defence they have assumed responsibility, together with home-based units necessary for the maintenance and relief of such forces.

(2) Member States may also recruit and maintain national armed forces for the fulfilment of international missions accepted by them, in Berlin, in Austria or in virtue of decisions of the United Nations. On conclusion of these missions such

troops shall either be dissolved or made available to the Community. The troops may be relieved, with the agreement of the competent Supreme Commander responsible to the North Atlantic Treaty Organization, by exchanges with units composed of contingents from the Member State concerned and belonging to the European Defence Forces.

(3) The troops in each State intended for the personal protection of the Head of the State shall remain national.

(4) Member States may dispose of national naval forces, on the one hand for the protection of the non-European territories for which they have assumed the defence responsibilities referred to in paragraph 1 of this Article and for the protection of communications with and between these territories and, on the other hand, for fulfilling the obligations arising out of the international missions referred to in paragraph 2 of this Article and of agreements concluded within the framework of the North Atlantic Treaty prior to the entry into force of the present Treaty.

(5) The total size of the national armed forces referred to in the present Article, including maintenance units, shall not be so large as to jeopardize the contribution of any Member State to the European Defence Forces, as determined by agreement between the Governments of the Member States.

Member States may carry out individual exchanges of personnel between the contingents which they place at the disposal of the European Defence Forces and the forces which do not form part thereof, provided that there is no consequent reduction in the size of the European Defence Forces.

Article 11. Police and gendarmerie forces, exclusively intended for the maintenance of internal order, may be recruited and maintained within Member States.

The national character of such forces is not affected by the present Treaty.

The size and nature of such forces on the territories of Member States shall not be such as to exceed the requirements of their mission.

Article 12. (1) In the event of disorders or threatened disorders within the territory of a Member State in Europe, the portion of the contingent made available by the State concerned to the

European Defence Forces and necessary for meeting this situation may, at its request and on notification to the Council, be placed at its disposal by the Board of Commissioners.

The conditions under which these units may be employed shall be as defined by the regulations in force within the territory of the Member State making the request.

(2) In the event of disaster or catastrophe requiring immediate assistance, the units of the European Defence Forces in a position to take useful action shall, regardless of their country of origin, lend their assistance.

Article 13. In the event of a major crisis affecting a non-European territory for whose defence a Member State has assumed responsibility, the portion of the contingents made available by the Member State concerned to the European Defence Forces and necessary to meet the crisis shall be, at its request and with the agreement of the competent Supreme Commander responsible to the North Atlantic Treaty Organization, placed at its disposal by the Board of Commissioners after notification to the Council. The contingents thus detached shall cease to be responsible to the Community until they are once again made available to it on being no longer needed to meet the crisis.

The military, economic and financial implications of the withdrawal provided for above shall in each case be examined and settled by the Board of Commissioners, with the approval of the Council acting on a two-thirds majority . . .

Article 15. (1) The European Defence Forces shall be made up of personnel recruited by conscription, of regular personnel or volunteer, long-service personnel.

(2) They shall wear a common uniform . . .

Article 16. The internal defence of the territories of Member States against attacks of any kind with military objectives, instigated or launched by an external enemy, shall be assured by homogeneous formations of European status, specialized for each Member State in the task of defending its territory, and depending for their employment on the authorities laid down in Article 18 below.

Article 17. Civil protection shall be the responsibility of each Member State individually.

Article 18. (1) The competent Supreme Commander responsible to the North Atlantic Treaty Organization shall, subject to the proviso in paragraph 3 below, be authorized to ensure that the European Defence Forces are organized, equipped, trained and prepared for their duties in a satisfactory manner.

As soon as they are ready for service, these Forces, subject to the proviso referred to above, shall be placed at the disposal of the competent Supreme Commander responsible to the North Atlantic Treaty Organization who shall exercise over them such authority and responsibilities as devolve on him by virtue of his mandate and, in particular, shall submit to the Community his requirements as regards the articulation and deployment of the Forces; the corresponding plans shall be carried out as specified in Article 77 below.

The European Defence Forces shall receive technical directives from the appropriate bodies of the North Atlantic Treaty Organization, within the framework of the military competence of the latter.

(2) In time of war, the competent Supreme Commander responsible to the North Atlantic Treaty Organization shall exercise over the Forces referred to above the full powers and responsibilities as Supreme Commander conferred upon him by his mandate.

(3) In the case of units of the European Defence Forces assigned to internal defence and the protection of the sea approaches of the territories of Member States, determination of the authorities to whom they shall be subordinate for Command purposes and employment shall depend either on NATO conventions concluded within the framework of the North Atlantic Treaty or on agreements between NATO and the Community.

4. Should the North Atlantic Treaty terminate before the present Treaty, it shall be the responsibility of the Member States to determine, by mutual agreement, the authority to whom the Command and employment of the European Defence Forces shall be assigned.

PART II. THE INSTITUTIONS OF THE COMMUNITY

Chapter I. The Board of Commissioners

Article 19. To enable the Board of Commissioners to carry out the duties laid on it under the present Treaty and under the conditions set forth therein, the Board of Commissioners shall be vested with executive and supervisory powers. The Board of Commissioners shall assume its responsibilities as soon as members have been nominated.

Article 20. (1) The Board of Commissioners shall be composed of nine members appointed for six years and chosen for their general qualifications.

Only nationals of Member States may be members of the Board of Commissioners, which shall not include more than two nationals of the same State.

Outgoing members may be reappointed.

The number of members of the Board of Commissioners may be reduced by decision of the Council acting unanimously.

In the accomplishment of their duties, the members of the Board of Commissioners shall neither ask for nor receive instructions from any Government. They shall refrain from any action inconsistent with the supranational character of their duties.

Each Member State shall undertake to respect this supranational character and to take no action calculated to influence the members of the Board of Commissioners in the performance of their duties.

The members of the Board of Commissioners may not exercise any other professional activity during the period of their service.

For a period of three years from the termination of his service no former Commissioner may exercise a professional activity which the Court, informed by him or by the Council, may deem owing to its connection with his former duties, to be incompatible with the obligations deriving from such duties. In the event of any breach of this provision, the Court may order the forfeiture of the pension rights of the individual concerned.

Article 21. (1) The members of the Board of Commissioners shall be appointed by agreement between the Governments of the Member States.

(2) The members appointed for the first time after the entry

into force of the present Treaty shall remain in office for a period of three years from the date of their appointment . . .

(3) On the expiry of the initial period of three years, a general renewal of membership shall take place.

(4) Membership of the Board of Commissioners shall be partially renewed thereafter by one-third every two years . . .

Article 36. (1) The Board of Commissioners shall submit each year a general report on its work to the Assembly one month before the opening of the ordinary session. The Assembly shall discuss the report and may make comments, express wishes and put forward suggestions.

(2) If the Assembly is seized of a motion of censure on the administration of the Board of Commissioners, it may not take a decision on the motion until three days at least have elapsed after its submission, and then only by a roll call vote.

Should the motion of censure be adopted by a two-thirds majority of the votes cast and by a majority of the members of the Assembly, the members of the Board of Commissioners shall collectively resign. They shall continue to deal with current business until steps have been taken to replace them under the conditions laid down in Article 21 above . . .

Article 38. (1) Within the period laid down in the second paragraph of this Article, the Assembly shall study:

- (*a*) the constitution of an Assembly of the European Defence Community, elected on a democratic basis;
- (*b*) the powers which would devolve on such an Assembly;
- (*c*) any changes which might have eventually to be made to the provisions of the present Treaty concerning the other institutions of the Community, particularly with a view to safeguarding an appropriate representation of States.

The Assembly will be particularly guided in its study by the following principles:

The final organization which will replace the present provisional organization should be so conceived as to be able to constitute one of the elements in a subsequent federal or confederal structure, based on the principle of the separation of powers and having, in particular, a two-chamber system of representation.

The Assembly shall also examine problems arising from the co-existence of different agencies for European co-operation already established or which might be established, with a view to ensuring co-ordination within the framework of the federal or confederal structure . . .

Chapter III. The Council

Article 39. (1) The general task of the Council shall be to harmonize the activities of the Board of Commissioners with the policies of the Governments of Member States.

(2) The Council may issue directives within the framework of the Treaty to guide the activities of the Board of Commissioners.

These directives shall be agreed unanimously.

With respect to questions on which the Council has not had occasion to issue directives, the Board of Commissioners may take action with a view to achieving the objectives laid down by the present Treaty, under the conditions defined herein.

(3) In accordance with the provisions of the present Treaty, the Council:

(*a*) shall take decisions;

(*b*) shall give the approval which the Board of Commissioners must obtain before taking decisions or making recommendations.

(4) Unless the present Treaty provides otherwise, the decisions and approval of the Council shall require a simple majority.

(5) When the Council is consulted by the Board of Commissioners, its deliberations need not be followed by a vote. The records of the discussions shall be transmitted to the Board of Commissioners.

Article 40. The Council shall be composed of representatives of the Member States.

Each Member State shall delegate to the Council a member of its Government; he may be represented by a Deputy.

The Council shall be so constituted as to be able to function at any time. To this end each Member State should have a permanent representative on the Council in a position to take part at any time in its discussions.

Following the alphabetical order of the Member States, each member of the Council shall in turn assume the Chairmanship for a period of three months.

Article 41. The Council shall meet as often as necessary and at least once every three months. It shall be convened by its Chairman, either on his own initiative or at the request of a member of the Council or of the Board of Commissioners . . .

Article 43. (1) In cases where the present Treaty requires approval or decision by the Council by a simple majority, the approval or the decision shall be obtained if the voting in its favour is as follows:

> either an absolute majority of the Representatives of Member States;
> or, where there is a tie-vote, a majority of the Representatives of Member States which, together, make available to the Community at least two-thirds of the total contributions of Member States.

(2) Where the present Treaty requires an approval or decision by the Council by a specified majority, the approval or decision shall be obtained:

> either by the majority thus defined, if such majority includes the votes of the Representatives of Member States which together make available to the Community two-thirds of the total contributions of Member States;
> or if they obtain the votes of five Member States.

(3) Where the present Treaty requires a unanimous approval or decision by the Council, the approval or decision shall be obtained if the votes in its favour include those of all the members present or represented on the Council; abstentions shall not prevent the adoption of the approval or decision.

(4) In paragraphs 1 and 2 above, the word 'contributions' shall be taken as the mean between the percentage of the financial contributions actually paid during the previous financial year and the percentage of manpower composing the European Defence Forces on the first day of the current half-year . . .

PART III. MILITARY PROVISIONS

Chapter I. Organization and Administration of the European Defence Forces

Article 68. (1) The basic units, in which the operational functions of the various Arms of the Land Forces will have to be combined, shall be composed of elements of the same nationality. These basic units shall be as small as is compatible with the principle of effectiveness. They shall be free, to the greatest possible extent of logistical functions and shall depend for their support and maintenance on higher integrated echelons.

(2) The Army Corps shall be composed of basic units of different nationalities, apart from exceptional cases resulting from tactical or organizational requirements determined by the Board of Commissioners on the proposal of the competent Supreme Commander responsible to the North Atlantic Treaty Organization and with the unanimous approval of the Council. Their tactical support units and the logistical support formations shall be of the integrated type; these latter elementary units, corresponding to a regiment or a battalion, shall remain homogeneous and their division by nationalities shall be in the same proportion as that obtaining in the basic units. The command and the General Staff of the Army Corps shall be integrated; this integration shall be carried out in the method best adapted to ensure their effective use.

(3) The basic units and their supporting services may from time to time be introduced into the North Atlantic Treaty Organization Army Corps and conversely, the North Atlantic Treaty Organization divisions may be introduced into the European Army Corps.

The Command echelons of the North Atlantic Treaty Organization Forces to which the European units shall be organically attached shall integrate the elements coming from these units and conversely.

Article 69. (1) The basic units of the Air Forces, each of which shall be supplied with homogeneous combat equipment corresponding to a single specific tactical task, shall be made up of elements of the same nationality.

These basic units shall be free to the greatest possible extent of logistical functions and shall depend for their use and maintenance on higher integrated echelons.

(2) A certain number of basic units of different nationalities shall be grouped under the orders of higher echelons of an integrated type, apart from exceptional cases resulting from tactical or organizational requirements determined by the Board of Commissioners on the proposal of the competent Supreme Commander responsible to the North Atlantic Treaty Organization and with the unanimous approval of the Council. The logistical support formations shall be of the integrated type the elementary service units remaining of homogeneous national composition and their division by nationalities shall be in the same proportion as that obtaining in the basic units.

(3) European basic units and their support units may be introduced into the North Atlantic Treaty Organization commands and, conversely, the basic North Atlantic Treaty Organization units may be introduced into the European Commands.

The North Atlantic Treaty Organization Command echelons to which the European units shall be organically attached shall integrate the European elements and conversely.

Article 70. (1) The European naval forces shall consist of such formations as may be required for the protection of the home waters of the European territories of Member States, as may be determined by agreement between the Governments concerned.

(2) Contingents to the European naval forces shall form groups of the same nationality and European status suitable for a single tactical task.

(3) These groups, in whole or in part, may from time to time be incorporated in formations responsible to the North Atlantic Treaty Organization, whose Command shall at once integrate the elements thus supplied . . .

PART V. ECONOMIC PROVISIONS

Article 101. The Board of Commissioners shall prepare, in consultation with the Governments of Member States, common programmes for the armament, equipment, supply and infrastructure of the European Defence Forces, and shall ensure, in conformity with Article 91 above, the execution of these programmes.

Article 102. (1) In preparing and carrying out the programmes, the Board of Commissioners shall:

(*a*) make the best possible use of the technical and economic capabilities of each of the Member States and avoid creating serious disturbances in their economies;

(*b*) take account of the size of the contributions to be made by Member States and respect the rules for the transfer of funds embodied in the Treaty;

(*c*) in co-operation with the appropriate NATO institutions, simplify and standardize armaments, equipment, supplies and infrastructure as much and as rapidly as possible.

(2) The Council may by a two-thirds majority give general instructions to the Board of Commissioners within the framework of the principles outlined above . . .

Article 104. . . . (3) Contracts shall be placed after the widest possible tenders have been asked for, except in cases justified for reasons of military secrecy or for technical reasons or on the grounds of urgency . . .

Article 106. The Board of Commissioners shall prepare a common programme of scientific and technical research in the military sphere, together with detailed plans for its execution. The programme shall be submitted to the Council for approval in the same way as the common programmes for armaments, equipment, supply and infrastructure of the European Defence Forces.

The Board of Commissioners shall ensure that the common research programme is put into effect.

Article 107. The production, import and export of war materials from or to third countries, measures directly concerning establishments intended for the production of war materials, and the manufacture of prototypes and technical research concerning war materials shall be forbidden, except as permitted [by the Board of Commissioners] . . .

Article 128. The present Treaty shall be concluded for a period of 50 years from its entry into force.

If, before the establishment of a European federation or

confederation, the North Atlantic Treaty should cease to be in force or there should be an essential modification of the membership of the North Atlantic Treaty Organization, the High Contracting Parties shall examine together the new situation thus created.

Article 129. Any European State may ask to accede to the present Treaty. The Council, after having taken the opinion of the Board of Commissioners shall take its decision, acting unanimously, and shall determine, also acting unanimously, the conditions for accession. Accession shall take effect from the day on which the instrument of accession is received by the Government depositary of the present Treaty . . .

DOCUMENT 5. EXTRACTS FROM THE DRAFT TREATY EMBODYING THE STATUTE OF THE EUROPEAN COMMUNITY ADOPTED BY THE *ad hoc* ASSEMBLY, 11 MARCH 1953

PREAMBLE

We, the Peoples of the Federal Republic of Germany, the Kingdom of Belgium, the French Republic, the Italian Republic, the Grand Duchy of Luxembourg and the Kingdom of the Netherlands,

Considering that world peace may be safeguarded only by creative efforts equal to the dangers which menace it;

Convinced that the contribution which a living, united and free Europe can bring to civilization and to the preservation of our common spiritual heritage is indispensable to the maintenance of peaceful relations;

Desirous of assisting through the expansion of our production in improving the standard of living and furthering the works of peace;

Determined to safeguard by our common action the dignity, freedom and fundamental equality of men of every condition, race or creed;

Resolved to substitute for our historic rivalries a fusion of our essential interests by creating institutions capable of giving guidance to our future common destiny;

Determined to invite other European peoples, imbued with the same ideal, to join with us in our endeavour;

Have decided to create a European Community.

Wherefore our respective Governments, through their Plenipotentiaries, meeting in the city of . . ., with powers found in good and due form, have adopted the present Treaty.

PART I. THE EUROPEAN COMMUNITY

Article 1. The present Treaty sets up a European Community of a supranational character.

The Community is founded upon a union of peoples and States, upon respect for their personality and upon equal rights and duties for all. It shall be indissoluble.

Article 2. The Community has the following mission and general aims:

— to contribute towards the protection of human rights and fundamental freedoms in Member States;

— to co-operate with the other free nations in ensuring the security of Member States against all aggression;

— to ensure the co-ordination of the foreign policy of Member States in questions likely to involve the existence, the security or the prosperity of the Community;

— to promote, in harmony with the general economy of Member States, the economic expansion, the development of employment and the improvement of the standard of living in Member States, by means, in particular, of the progressive establishment of a common market, transitional or other measures being taken to ensure that no fundamental and persistent disturbance is thereby caused to the economy of Member States;

— to contribute towards the endeavours of Member States to achieve the general objectives laid down in the Statute of the Council of Europe, the European Convention for Economic Co-operation, and the North Atlantic Treaty, in co-operation with the other States parties thereto.

Article 3. The provisions of Part 1 of the Convention for the Protection of Human Rights and Fundamental Freedoms signed in Rome on 4 November 1950, together with those of the Protocol signed in Paris on 20 March 1952 are an integral part of the present Statute.

Article 4. The Community shall have juridical personality . . .

Article 5. The Community, together with the European Coal and Steel Community and the European Defence Community, shall constitute a single legal entity, within which certain organs may retain such administrative and financial autonomy as is necessary to the accomplishment of the tasks assigned by the treaties instituting the European Coal and Steel Community and the European Defence Community.

Article 6. The Community shall exercise all such powers and such competence as are conferred upon it by the present Statute or by subsequent enactment.

The provisions defining the powers and competence conferred upon the Community by the present Treaty shall be restrictively interpreted . . .

PART II. THE INSTITUTIONS OF THE COMMUNITY

Article 9. The institutions of the Community shall be:
— Parliament;
— the European Executive Council;
— the Council of National Ministers;
— the Court of Justice, hereinafter termed 'the Court';
— the Economic and Social Council.

Chapter I. Parliament

Article 10. Parliament shall enact legislation and make recommendations and proposals. It shall also approve the budget and pass a bill approving the accounts[1] of the Community. It shall exercise such powers of supervision as are conferred upon it by the present Statute.

Article 11. Parliament shall be composed of two Chambers which, unless the present Statute otherwise provides, shall have identical powers and competence.

The first Chamber, entitled the Peoples' Chamber, shall be composed of deputies representing the peoples united in the Community.

The second Chamber, entitled the Senate, shall be composed of senators representing the people of each State.

[1] La loi des comptes.

Article 12. Deputies and senators shall vote as individuals and in person.

They may not accept any mandate as to the way in which they shall cast their votes.

Article 13. Deputies shall be elected by universal, equal and direct suffrage, by secret ballot open to both men and women.

The Community shall enact legislation defining the principles of the electoral system.

Article 14. The Peoples' Chamber shall be elected for five years, subject to the provisions of Article 31, paragraphs (4) and (5).

Article 15. The peoples united in the Community shall be represented in the Peoples' Chamber in accordance with the following conditions:

(1) The number of deputies elected from the territory of a Member State may not be less than 12 nor more than 70.

(2) An equal number of deputies shall be elected from the territories of Germany, France and Italy. Additional representation shall, however, be granted to the French Republic in order to take into account its oversea departments and territories, under conditions to be laid down by French legislation.

An equal number of deputies shall be elected from the territories of Belgium and the Netherlands.

(3) The number of deputies elected from the territories of the Member States shall be as follows:

Germany	63
Belgium	30
France	70
Italy	63
Luxembourg	12
Netherlands	30

Article 16. (1) Senators shall be elected by the national Parliaments for five years in accordance with the procedure determined by each Member State . . .

Article 17. The number of senators shall be as follows:

Germany	21
Belgium	10

France .	.	.	.	.	21
Italy .	.	.	.	.	21
Luxembourg .	.	.	.	4
Netherlands .	.	.	.	10

Article 18. Each Chamber of Parliament shall verify the regularity of the election of its members.

Article 19. The Community shall enact legislation determining the conditions of eligibility for membership of Parliament.

Article 20. (1) Membership of the European Parliament shall not be confined to members of national Parliaments . . .

Chapter II. The European Executive Council

Article 27. The European Executive Council shall undertake the general administration of the Community. It shall have no powers other than those conferred upon it by the present Statute.

Article 28. The Senate shall elect the President of the European Executive Council in secret ballot, by majority vote of its members.

(2) The President shall appoint the other members of the European Executive Council.

(3) The European Executive Council shall not include more than two members of the same nationality.

(4) The members of the European Executive Council shall have the title of Ministers of the European Community.

Article 29. Only nationals of Member States may be members of the European Executive Council.

Article 30. (1) The office of a member of the European Executive Council shall be incompatible with that of a member of the Government of a participating State, of a judge or solicitor-general in the Court or of a member of the Economic and Social Council.

(2) Members of the European Executive Council may not exercise any paid function. They may belong neither to the management nor to the Board of Directors of any enterprise conducted for profit.

Article 31. (1) The European Executive Council shall assume its functions as soon as its composition has been published in the Official Journal of the Community. It shall forthwith request the Peoples' Chamber and the Senate for a vote of confidence, which shall be given by each Chamber by majority vote of its members.

(2) The European Executive Council shall remain in office until the end of the life of the current Peoples' Chamber. It shall resign from office notwithstanding, if a vote of no confidence is passed against it by the Peoples' Chamber or the Senate. It shall also be required to resign if the Peoples' Chamber or the Senate refuses to grant its request for a vote of confidence.

(3) The Senate shall be deemed to have passed a vote of no confidence in the European Executive Council if it elects a new President, under the provisions of the first paragraph of Article 28.

The Peoples' Chamber shall require for a vote of no confidence in the European Executive Council a three-fifths majority vote of its members.

Subject to the provisions of paragraph (1) of the present article, the withholding of a vote of confidence, if it is to be effective, must take place under the same conditions as a vote of no confidence.

(4) If a motion of no confidence, or alternatively the withholding of a vote of confidence which has been requested of the Peoples' Chamber by the European Executive Council, is voted by a majority of less than three-fifths of the members of the Chamber, it shall be at the discretion of the European Executive Council either to resign or to declare the Chamber dissolved.

Such dissolution may not be ordered until after the expiry of a period of five clear days. The instrument of dissolution shall include convocation of the electoral body of the Peoples' Chamber within a period of forty days, and of the Chamber within two months.

The withholding of a vote of confidence by the Peoples' Chamber shall not, however, entail the option of dissolving the Chamber in the case mentioned in paragraph (1) of the present Article.

(5) The right of the European Executive Council to order the dissolution of the Peoples' Chamber, in implementation of

the preceding paragraph, shall lapse if, within the period determined in that paragraph, the Senate passes a vote of no confidence in the European Executive Council under the conditions laid down in paragraph (3) of the present Article.

(6) The President of the European Executive Council shall tender the resignation of the Council to the President of the Senate. The retiring Council shall conduct current business until its successor takes up office.

(7) The members of the European Executive Council shall resign in a body if and when the President ceases to exercise his functions.

Article 32. The President of the European Executive Council may dismiss or replace any member of that Council, subject to the approval of the Peoples' Chamber and the Senate.

Article 33. In order to fulfil the tasks entrusted to it, and in accordance with the conditions laid down in the present Statute, the European Executive Council shall take decisions, make recommendations or express opinions.

Decisions shall be binding in all respects.

Recommendations shall have binding effect with regard to the aims specified therein, but shall leave the means of implementation to the Authorities to whom the recommendation is addressed.

Opinions shall not be binding.

Article 34. The President of the European Executive Council shall represent the Community in international relations.

Chapter III. The Council of National Ministers

Article 35. The Council of National Ministers shall exercise its powers and competence in the cases specified and in the manner indicated in the present Statute with a view to harmonizing the action of the European Executive Council with that of the Governments of Member States.

The Council of National Ministers and the European Executive Council shall exchange information and consult each other.

Article 36. The Council of National Ministers shall be composed of representatives of the Member States. Each State shall delegate a member of its Government as a representative.

The Chairmanship shall be taken by each of the Members of the Council in turn for a period of three months, in accordance with the alphabetical order of the names of the Member States.

Article 37. The Council of National Ministers shall be convened by its Chairman at the request of a Member State or the European Executive Council.

The Council of National Ministers shall communicate with each Member State through the Minister representing the latter.

Chapter IV. The Court

Article 38. (1) The Court shall ensure the rule of law in the interpretation and application of the present Statute and of the laws and regulations of the Community.

(2) The Court of the Community shall be identical with the Court of the European Coal and Steel Community and of the European Defence Community, thus ensuring unity of jurisprudence.

(3) Other courts set up by existing or subsequent treaties shall assist the Court in the exercise of its functions.

Article 39. (1) The number of judges shall not exceed fifteen.

(2) They shall be selected from a double list by the European Executive Council, acting with the approval of the Senate. Each Member State may put forward three candidates; the national groups of the Permanent Arbitration Court in each Member State shall be entitled to exercise a similar right . . .

Chapter V. The Economic and Social Council

Article 50. The Economic and Social Council shall assist the European Executive Council and Parliament in an advisory capacity.

It shall deliver opinions to each of the Chambers of Parliament and the European Executive Council, if they so request. It may also transmit resolutions to them . . .

Chapter VI. Legislation

Article 52. (1) The passing of legislation shall require the assent of each of the two Chambers in succession by simple majority . . .

PART III

Chapter V. Economic powers

Article 82. The Community, while upholding the principles defined in Articles 2, 3 and 4 of the Treaty instituting the European Coal and Steel Community, shall establish progressively a common market among the Member States, based on the free movement of goods, capital and persons.

In order to achieve the aim mentioned in the preceding paragraph, the Community shall foster the co-ordination of the policy of the Member States in monetary, credit and financial matters . . .

DOCUMENT 6. EXTRACTS FROM THE SPEECH BY M. EDOUARD HERRIOT IN THE NATIONAL ASSEMBLY, 30 AUGUST 1954

What's the good of a great Assembly like yours laying down conditions and then throwing them in the fire and saying that they were just a joke, they were just meant to make an impression abroad? There are at least two conditions which have been sacrificed. First of all the Saar: perhaps there are some talks going on about this at the moment, but they are family secrets that we know nothing about. And then above all I would say there is the British condition which has not been fulfilled [applause]. I declare—I don't have the right to say: with all the authority of my career behind me—but with the conviction of a man who has always believed that no international negotiation for peace and freedom can possibly do without the basic agreement of France and Britain, nations which are not alike but are complementary, nations which each by their different means safeguard that peace and that liberty [applause] . . . Nothing supports (and you know that this is one of the essential concerns of the government) the notion that Britain is committed by our side in a matter of which—one may say without exaggeration—that to stand up against the power and, if I may say so, the possible intrigues of Germany, no alliance can be too close with the same risks, the same responsibilities between the United Kingdom and France [applause]. This absence of solidarity or even of declared solidarity between France and Britain is one reason which

I believe would by itself make me reject the Defence Community . . .

But, ladies and gentlemen, we have other reasons to oppose this European Defence Community: we have alas only too many arguments. But the essential one is, I believe, that of the diminution of the sovereignty and of the independence of our country ['Hear, hear' from the extreme right]. Allow me to be particularly emphatic on this point because at my age this is one's deepest opinion and it is also the dearest wish of our whole national consciousness [applause on many benches of the left and of the extreme right]. My dear colleagues, I think I shall have no difficulty in showing that the EDC Treaty will make Germany take a leap towards sovereignty [interruption by M. Gaston Defferre: 'She'll do that in any case!'] and at the same time make France leap backwards where her own independence and her own sovereignty are concerned . . .

And what are these diminutions in sovereignty for France? To quote only the chief ones, I believe they are: firstly, that her army is cut in two. No one can deny that; secondly, that the length of military service is not fixed by the National Parliament [cries from the centre: 'That's not true!']; thirdly, that the budget of the armies is voted by unanimity in the Council and then divided . . . fourthly, that pay will be fixed by the Commission; fifthly, that Generals will no longer be appointed by the President of the Republic; lastly, that mobilization will be partly out of our hands. And so I ask you: when a people is no longer in charge of its own army is it still in charge of its diplomacy? And I answer: No, it no longer is . . .

And if anyone wanted to deny how humiliating these restrictions are on our country in the first place and how serious in their consequences then I would ask you to look at Article 20 of the Paris Treaty which consecrates all these surrenders, all these restrictions, because it says: 'In the accomplishment of their duties the Members of the Board of Commissioners shall neither ask for nor receive instructions from any government. They shall refrain from any action inconsistent with the supranational character of their duties.' So these Commissioners are to be completely cut off, the text is very clear on this point, from all relations with their own

countries [interruption: 'That's what is called European'].
Well, I say that this text is both monstrous and ridiculous
[applause from the far left, the far right and from many
benches of the left and some on the right]. What real French-
man would ever agree to represent his country under such
conditions? [applause]. This is monstrous and ridiculous
because it means putting a premium on those who are not
loyal. I believe that within the Atlantic Community there will
certainly be found representatives who, in spite of all the texts
will, as they have done in the past, put the defence of their own
country first, the defence of their mother country even perhaps
in spite of the letter of the law . . . What would these Commissioners be? Abstract beings, superhuman beings or some
kind of robots by whom we shall be governed, directed,
ordered about . . .

But, ladies and gentlemen, quite apart from this national
humiliation which no revolutionary assembly, no Republican
assembly would ever have put up with [applause from the
extreme left, the extreme right, and many benches of the left],
what will happen to Germany? . . . M. Bidault declared on
4 February 1954: '. . . I think it is impossible to sustain any
longer the thesis according to which a future Germany would
not be a free Germany and would be bound by undertakings
entered into by the Federal German Republic.' Thus according
to a French Minister—and what a respectable one at that—a
united Germany would be perfectly free . . . In leaving Germany free, in giving her everything one could possibly have
given her—for I don't see what more she could have asked for
at the moment [interruption from the centre: 'The *Wehrmacht*!']
there is only one country towards which you have left her
free: that country is Russia, with whom she can then negotiate
as she wishes—and a country that will have its hands full of
possible rewards to give in exchange. Thus my dear colleagues—
and I tell you this from the very bottom of my intellect—the
EDC Treaty will throw Germany into the arms of the Russians
[applause on many benches of the left and of the extreme right
and some benches of the right, interruptions from the centre,
and various voices on the right calling to the extreme left:
'Go on and vote for ratification!']. I do not look to the left or
to the right, I am looking straight ahead of me as I have done

for all my life [applause]. If I have my eyes on anything it is only the interest of my country. At my age one no longer thinks of anything else [applause] . . . It is only reasonable to reply that if Germany has the right of withdrawing, then France must have the same right . . . I ask you: do you really want to accept this discrimination against France and not against Germany? It is up to you to reply. As for me, my conscience has already given the answer . . .

It is better to speak out frankly. The conflict between us is not a conflict of form, not a conflict of detail, it is a conflict of principle ['Hear, hear' from the extreme right]. For us the European Community, let me say this as I believe it, on the far edge of my life, summarizing in this conviction all the efforts that I have been able to make: for me, for us, the European Community is the end of France [applause]. Perhaps it would not be the end of France if it were with a country that had not already several times deceived us. But we have known and we have suffered from that country such departures from legality that I am entitled, I who am an old man, I who am about to disappear, to tell you lovingly, not threateningly, but from the bottom of my heart: beware, so that you do not have to regret an act that you can never make up for, an act that you can never undo . . .

We are divided on the very principle of the problem and so it is better to settle the question and to let this abscess disappear from French political life. You are sincere, I am certain of it, but we are older than you and, alas, we have seen so much [interruption: 'We don't want to see such things again'] . . . For us this is the question of the life or death of France . . .

And let me tell you where I believe the real heart of the matter, the crux of the discussion lies. You see, my dear colleagues, you will never find peace by looking for it on the paths of war [applause]. We do not want a solution by arms, by rearmament, by overarmament [M. Jules Moch: 'Hear, hear']. We want a solution for a united Europe, for the whole of Europe if that is possible, and not just for a Europe of five or six . . . and moreover we have with the Russians a Treaty which commits us to a certain extent and if you tell me 'Ah, we know you, you want an alliance with the Russians' then I would reply: at my age I want nothing more except to see my country commit herself on the path which will lead her to relative happiness, but really I do not see why one should not look for an appeasement, an agreement, a settlement [interruption from M. Jean Legendre: 'Like in 1939!'] with those who have already helped us in tragic hours and we have but to ask them to let us know a little more about their attitude and to offer us their collaboration a little more clearly.

Ladies and gentlemen, let me add several arguments which I think essential: first of all Article 11 of the Treaty says that Germany will be allowed to set up police and gendarmerie forces . . . So if tomorrow you see a Gestapo or an SS reconstituted, don't be too surprised. As for me, I will not forget that if in the German Army there remained some elements of honour, at least of professional honour, that army in its occupation of France was accompanied by real hangmen who massacred my brothers, and that I want never to forget [applause].

And then this Community army will be absolutely useless . . . An army must have a soul ['Hear, hear']. What is the army of a country? It is not the mathematical addition of its conscripts, it is the country itself rallied round its flag for the defence of its material and intellectual treasures, for the defence of its liberty, of its independence, and it is just because these feelings, developed by the French Revolution (no one can deny it) run so deep in our country, that they gave to the men on the Marne the courage to die in conditions which we must never forget [applause]. The army, that is the soul of the Fatherland and I would well like to know where the army of the Community would find its soul . . .

This is an adventure in which you must not allow yourselves to be involved. A great country like France must stand above such things. Let us work to give her her moral force, her cohesion, her strength, do not let us divide her and do not let us believe that France in her present state is more in danger than that France that you want to send back to Brussels to play her role in the international concert where we have just seen how our old country, our Republic, is treated when she seems about to give up her rights [interruptions], her sovereignty, and her independence.

DOCUMENT 7. EXTRACTS FROM A REPORT OF REMARKS MADE BY
DR. KONRAD ADENAUER IN LONDON 28 SEPTEMBER 1954, AS
PUBLISHED IN 'DER SPIEGEL' OF 6 OCTOBER 1954

'That I should be forced to set up a German National Army—
that's nonsense, Mr. Bech, that's grotesque' . . . Bech, Spaak
and Adenauer were a solitary group half-hidden behind the
columns in a corner of the great empty salon of London's
luxury hotel, Claridges . . . It was a few minutes before midnight on 28 September, the first day of the London Conference, of which Konrad Adenauer said a day later that its
failure was a catastrophe for Europe. The three Ministers had
sat down together for a last drink after coming back late from
Downing Street where Sir Winston Churchill had given a
dinner to the nine Ministers of Foreign Affairs and the Ambassadors of the eight Allied States; they were talking over the
events of the day as comrades sharing the same ideals—only
the fourth in their alliance in the battle for Europe, Holland's
Minister for Foreign Affairs Johan Beyen, was absent—he was
not staying at Claridges and had withdrawn tired to his own
quarters . . .

Thus Spaak and Bech witnessed an unusually violent
explosion of the Chancellor's deep bitterness which finally
subsided in depression. Konrad Adenauer saw his vision of
a larger combination of West European states, including a
part of Germany, which had determined his policy so far . . .
dissolve into the void. 'I am absolutely convinced, one hundred
per cent convinced that the German National Army which
Mendes France is forcing on us will be a great danger for
Germany and for Europe—when I'm no longer here I don't
know what is going to become of Germany unless we cannot
still somehow succeed in uniting Europe in time.'

Bech and Spaak were listening to Adenauer tense and un-
believing and the Luxembourg Minister countered that
France would see to it that the German Army would be kept
under control and not be made an instrument of a new German
nationalism. But Konrad Adenauer brushed the objections
aside with an impatient gesture: 'Don't rely on that, Mr. Bech.
It's a great error to count on France once the game of European
Nation States starts up again. The French nationalists are just

as ready as the German, in spite of all our bitter experiences, to repeat the old policy. They'd rather see Germany with its own National Army than Europe, provided only that they can make their own policy with the Russians. And the German nationalists think just the same way; they are ready to go with the Russians . . . If Europe is not united and Germany has a National Army then you can look out one day, Herr Bech, I'll tell you that now. If the nationalists get back to power in Germany . . .'

The fear of a resurgence of a cynically stupid German nationalism, which runs deep in Konrad Adenauer's mind, appeared to have taken hold of him completely. Again and again he raised his voice to implore his two listeners to believe him: 'Believe me, the danger of German nationalism is much bigger than people think. The crisis in European policy makes the nationalists daring; they are gaining in confidence and in support.' This nightmare which the wide-awake brain of this 78-year-old was imparting to his listeners became more and more oppressive at this witching hour. Konrad Adenauer spoke of the time after him. He did not speak about his death. His thoughts were beyond that point. He spoke with the passionate concern of a man who knows that time is running away from him. Again and again he used the words: 'when I've gone'. The whisky-soda had gone flat in its glass, its bubbles had long evaporated; Paul Henri Spaak was striking match after match to light his cigar up again which continually went out. 'Use the time while I'm alive, when I'm no longer here it will be too late—my God, I don't know what my successors will do if they are left to themselves, if they are not forced to move along rigidly pre-determined lines, if they are not tied to Europe.' . . .

'What we are doing here now must be no more than a transitional solution. We must not resign, we must not capitulate before nationalism, we must use the Brussels Treaty as a growth point for the European Defence Community, as a base from which to move to a political European Community and use every opportunity to get closer to our goal of the unity of Europe.' And deep in thought, he added: 'And there isn't much time left.' . . .

'Don't deceive yourselves, don't let yourselves be deceived, the danger is great, it's greater than ever if we give up now. Europe will have failed and everything was in vain, everything will remain in vain—everything will start again at the beginning with the rivalry and intrigues of nation states against each other and only Moscow will profit from that.' After those words nothing more could be heard from the corner table until a waiter interrupted the pensive silence with the words 'More ice, gentlemen?'

PART II

Economic and Political Community

DOCUMENT 8. RESOLUTION ADOPTED BY THE MINISTERS OF
FOREIGN AFFAIRS OF THE MEMBER STATES OF THE ECSC AT THEIR
MEETING AT MESSINA ON I AND 2 JUNE 1955

The Governments of the Federal Republic, Belgium, France, Italy, Luxembourg and the Netherlands believe that the time has come to make a fresh advance towards the building of Europe. They are of the opinion that this must be achieved, first of all, in the economic field.

They consider that it is necessary to work for the establishment of a united Europe by the development of common institutions, the progressive fusion of national economies, the creation of a common market and the progressive harmonization of their social policies.

Such a policy seems to them indispensable if Europe is to maintain her position in the world, regain her influence and prestige and achieve a continuing increase in the standard of living of her population.

I

To these ends, the six Ministers have agreed on the following objectives:

A. 1. The expansion of trade and the freedom of movement call for the joint development of the major channels of communication.

A joint study will accordingly be undertaken of development plans based on the establishment of a European network of canals, motor highways, electrified railways and on a standardization of equipment, as well as a study of possible means of achieving a better co-ordination of air transport.

2. A fundamental condition of economic progress is that the

European economies should have at their disposal cheaper and more plentiful supplies of power.

For this reason, all possible steps will have to be taken to develop exchanges of gas and electricity as necessary to increase the profitability of investment and to reduce the cost of supplies.

Study will be given to methods for co-ordinating a joint approach to questions affecting the future production and consumption of power, and for drawing up the general lines of an overall policy.

3. The development of atomic energy for peaceful purposes will in the near future open up the prospect of a new industrial revolution out of all proportion to that which has taken place over the last hundred years. The six signatory States consider that it is necessary to study the creation of a common organization to be entrusted with the responsibility and the means for ensuring the peaceful development of atomic energy, while taking into account the special arrangements made by certain Governments with third countries.

These means should comprise:

(a) The establishment of a common fund derived from contributions from each of the participating countries, from which provision could be made for financing the installations and research work already in progress or planned.

(b) Free and sufficient access to the raw materials, and the free exchange of expertise and technicians, by-products and specialized equipment.

(c) The pooling of the results obtained and the granting of financial assistance for their exploitation.

(d) Co-operation with non-member countries.

B. The six Governments recognize that the establishment of a European market, free from all customs duties and all quantitative restrictions, is the objective of their action in the field of economic policy.

They consider that this market must be achieved by stages and that its entry into force requires a study of the following questions:

(a) The appropriate procedure and pace for the progressive suppression of the obstacles to trade in the relations between the participating countries, as well as the appropriate measures for moving towards a progressive unification of their tariffs against third countries.

(*b*) The measures to be taken for harmonizing the general policy of the participating countries in the financial, economic and social fields.

(*c*) The adoption of methods designed to make possible an adequate co-ordination of the monetary policies of the member countries so as to permit the creation and development of a common market.

(*d*) A system of escape clauses.

(*e*) The creation and operation of a readaptation fund.

(*f*) The gradual introduction of the free movement of manpower.

(*g*) The elaboration of rules which would ensure the play of competition within the common market so as to exclude, in particular, all discrimination on a national basis.

(*h*) The institutional arrangements appropriate for introducing and operating the common market.

C. The creation of a European Investment Fund will be studied. The object of this fund would be the joint development of European economic potentialities and in particular the development of the less developed regions of the participating states.

D. As regards the social field, the six Governments consider it essential to study the progressive harmonization of the regulations in force in the different countries, notably those which concern working hours, overtime rates (night work, Sunday work and public holidays) and the length and rates of pay for holidays.

II

The six Governments have decided to adopt the following procedure:

(1) Conferences will be called to work out treaties or other arrangements concerning the questions under consideration.

(2) The preparatory work will be the responsibility of a Committee of Governmental representatives, assisted by

experts, under the chairmanship of a political personality responsible for co-ordinating the work in the different fields.

(3) The Committee will invite the High Authority of the ECSC and the Secretariats of OEEC, the Council of Europe and the European Conferences of Ministers of Transport, to give the necessary assistance.

(4) The report of the Committee, covering the whole field, will be submitted to the Ministers of Foreign Affairs by not later than the 1st of October, 1955.

(5) The Ministers for Foreign Affairs will meet before that date to take note of the interim reports prepared by the Committee and to give it the necessary directives.

(6) The Government of the United Kingdom, as a power which is a member of WEU and is also associated with the ECSC, will be invited to take part in this work.

(7) The Ministers for Foreign Affairs will decide in due course whether other States should subsequently be invited to take part in the conference or conferences referred to in paragraph (1) above.

THE CHIEF INSTITUTIONS OF THE EUROPEAN COMMUNITIES

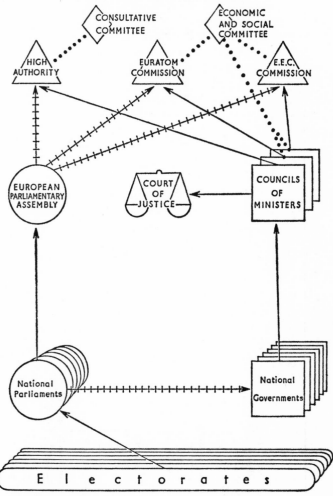

——▶ Appointment or election +++▶ Power of dismissal •••• Consultation

TABLE A: SOME COMPARISONS

	Germany	France	Italy	Netherlands	Belgium	Luxembourg	EEC	UK	USA
Area ('000 square miles)	96	213	131	35	12	1	488	94	3600
Population (millions, mid 1965)	59·0	48·9	51·6	12·3	9·5	0·3	181·6	54·6	192·6
Civilian labour force (millions 1965)	26·7	19·4	19·0	4·4	3·6	0·1	74	25	72
Percentage in agriculture	11	18	26	10	6	14	(17)	4	8
Percentage in industry	49	40	40	44	46	45	(43)	47	31
Percentage in services	39	41	33	46	48	41	(39)	48	55
Percentage unemployed	1	1	1	0	0	—	(1)	1	6
1965 gross national product at market prices ($'000m.)	112	94	57	19	17	..	300	99	692
1965 per capita GNP ($)	1900	1920	1100	1550	1780	..	..	1810	3560
Volume index of GNP 1964 (1958 = 100) 1965	141 147	137 142	143 148	137 146	131 138	.. ..	139 ..	126 ..	129 ..
Average annual growth rates of GNP at constant prices: 1953–58 1958–64	6·9 5·8	4·6 5·3	5·2 6·1	4·1 5·4	2·6 4·7	.. ..	5·3 5·6	2·2 3·9	1·7 4·3

74

	Germany	France	Italy	Netherlands	Belgium	Luxembourg	EEC	UK	USA
Actual annual rates of growth:									
1958	+ 3·2	+ 2·7	+ 5·0	— 0·1	— 1·0	..	+ 2·9	+ 0·9	— 0·9
1959	+ 7·0	+ 3·0	+ 6·3	+ 5·2	+ 2·6	..	+ 5·1	+ 4·0	+ 6·2
1960	+ 8·8	+ 7·4	+ 6·3	+ 8·9	+ 5·6	..	+ 7·7	+ 4·9	+ 2·4
1961	+ 5·4	+ 4·4	+ 8·2	+ 3·5	+ 4·7	..	+ 5·4	+ 3·5	+ 2·0
1962	+ 4·2	+ 7·1	+ 6·3	+ 3·8	+ 5·5	..	+ 5·6	+ 1·1	+ 6·5
1963	+ 3·4	+ 4·5	+ 5·1	+ 3·7	+ 4·6	..	+ 4·4	+ 4·4	+ 4·0
1964	+ 6·6	+ 6·0	+ 3·0	+ 8·8	+ 6·6	..	+ 5·8	+ 5·6	+ 5·3
1965	+ 4·6	+ 3·5	+ 3·9	+ 5·4	+ 3·3	..	+ 4·1	+ 2·4	+ 5·9
1966									
Private consumption as percentage of GNP 1958	59·5	65·8	65·6	58·6	68·3	60·3	63·3	66·4	64·0
1965	56·9	63·8	62·3	58·0	65·5	(62·1)	60·6	64·0	62·6
Public consumption as percentage of GNP 1958	13·2	13·4	12·3	14·4	11·9	12·8	13·1	16·0	18·6
1965	15·5	13·3	14·7	15·9	12·8	(12·4)	14·5	16·7	18·1
Gross fixed asset formation as percentage of GNP 1958	21·8	19·2	20·5	22·4	16·5	24·0	20·3	15·1	16·9
1965	26·6	21·7	18·9	24·5	20·7	(25·5)	23·1	17·7	17·2
Index of average hourly gross wages in industry 1966 (1958 = 100)	193	174	187*	190	159	152*	..	144	129
General index of consumer prices 1966 (1958 = 100)	122	136	132	133	120	115	..	126	112

Source for Tables A and B: *Statistical Bulletins* and *OECD Observer* ( ) Estimated. * 1965.

TABLE B: GENERAL INDICES OF INDUSTRIAL PRODUCTION

(Excluding building, food, beverages and tobacco)

(i) 1953 = 100

	Germany	France	Italy	Netherlands	Belgium	Luxembourg	The Six	UK	USA
1950	72	89	78	88	93	89	80	94	82
1951	85	99	89	91	106	99	92	98	89
1952	91	98	91	91	100	109	95	95	92
1953	100	100	100	100	100	100	100	100	100
1954	112	109	109	111	106	103	110	108	94
1955	129	117	119	119	116	116	122	114	106
1956	139	128	128	124	123	124	132	114	109
1957	147	139	138	127	124	126	140	116	110
1958	152	145	143	127	116	121	144	114	102

(ii) 1958 = 100

	Germany	France	Italy	Netherlands	Belgium	Luxembourg	EEC	UK	USA
1958	100	100	100	100	100	100	100	100	100
1959	108	101	111	111	105	104	106	105	114
1960	122	111	129	124	113	114	119	113	117
1961	129	117	145	130	119	117	127	113	118
1962	134	123	159	137	127	112	135	114	128
1963	139	130	173	144	137	113	142	119	135
1964	152	140	175	158	147	124	152	128	144
1965	161	142	184	169	150	125	158	132	157
1966	163	151	207	181	153	120	167	133	172

TABLE C: TRADE FIGURES
(all in $m. monthly averages)

	F.R. of Germany[1]	France[2]	Italy	Netherlands	BLEU[6]	EEC internal	EEC external	UK	USA
(i) Total exports									
1954	437	348	136	201	192	389	927	647	1259
1955	511	409	155	224	230	471	1059	706	1296
1956	613	379	179	238	264	536	1137	774	1591
1957	714	421	212	258	264	596	1274	807	1737
1958	734	427	215	268	254	572	1326	773	1493
1959	817	467	243	301	275	681	1421	806	1448
1960	951	572	304	336	315	854	1624	858	1692
1961	1057	602	349	359	327	991	1702	896	1720
1962	1105	614	389	382	360	1130	1720	922	1774
1963	1218	674	421	413	403	1327	1802	988	1910
1964	1351	749	497	484	466	1532	2015	1028	2174
1965	1491	837	599	533	532	1736	2257	1143	2250
1966	1678	908	669	563	569	1936	2451	1222	2492
1967									

For footnotes see p, 79.

(ii) Total imports

	F.R. of Germany	France	Italy	Netherlands	BLEU	EEC internal	EEC external	UK	USA
1954	381	351	203	239	212	387	1005	787	858
1955	483	395	226	267	235	464	1142	906	958
1956	551	463	264	310	273	528	1335	907	1064
1957	625	510	306	342	285	586	1482	950	1105
1958	614	467	268	302	261	566	1346	874	1105
1959	706	424	281	328	287	673	1350	931	1249
1960	842	523	394	378	330	846	1620	1063	1221
1961	912	556	435	426	352	976	1705	1026	1196
1962	1023	627	506	446	380	1118	1863	1048	1353
1963	1085	727	632	497	426	1311	2056	1125	1418
1964	1218	839	604	588	494	1504	2238	1287	1550
1965	1456	861	612	622	530	1701	2382	1345	1773
1966	1502	990	714	668	598	1910	2561	1389	2114
1967									

(iii) Imports from developing countries[4]

	F.R. of Germany	France	Italy	Netherlands	BLEU	EEC AOC & T[3]	others	UK	USA
1958	147	217	79	75	51	129	440	308	482
1959	162	185	81	73	54	113	443	:	:
1960	188	202	95	75	63	139	485	336	490
1961	194	202	16	79	61	148	483	321	461
1962	213	217	113	78	59	154	526	329	497
1963	220	227	137	84	66	159	576	364	502
1964	251	247	147	98	77	172	648	365	582
1965	280	252	165	100	80	170	707	370	598

	F.R. of Germany[5]	France	Italy	Netherlands	BLEU	EEC	UK	USA
(iv) Imports from Eastern Europe including USSR								
1958	22	14	9	6	5	56	24	5
1959	26	13	10	5	5	59	17	8
1960	37	13	22	8	6	81	32	7
1961	34	14	26	9	7	90	36	7
1962	39	16	28	8	8	100	37	7
1963	38	21	35	10	9	114	40	7
1964	41	22	31	10	10	113	43	8
1965	49	23	37	13	10	131	51	11
1966	54	29	43	13	11	150	56	14
1967								

[1] Including the Saar from 6.7.1959.
[2] Excluding the Saar from 6.7.1959.
[3] Associated Overseas Countries and Territories.
[4] Countries other than: Europe, Northern America, Australia, New Zealand, Union of South Africa, Japan, Mainland China, North Vietnam, Outer Mongolia, North Korea.
[5] Excluding 'intra-zonal' trade between East and West Germany.
[6] Belgio-Luxembourg Economic Union.
Source: OECD *General Statistics*.

(V) UNITED KINGDOM GENERAL EXPORTS

	EEC	EFTA	OStgA	USA	World
1958	108	77	310	69	783
1959	119	84	290	89	806
1960	131	92	309	80	858
1961	155	104	299	70	896
1962	182	111	284	82	922
1963	208	121	306	85	988
1964	225	134	322	100	1065
1965	229	143	345	121	1143
1966	243	160	375	152	1122
1967					

(VI) UNITED KINGDOM GENERAL IMPORTS

	EEC	EFTA	OStgA	USA	World
1958	125	86	295	82	882
1959	131	92	312	87	931
1960	155	109	324	132	1063
1961	158	108	308	113	1026
1962	165	108	316	111	1048
1963	180	118	353	117	1125
1964	220	147	396	152	1329
1965	232	156	381	157	1345
1966	258	168	420	169	1389
1967					

OStgA = Overseas Sterling Area.

TABLE D: GROSS RESERVES OF GOLD AND CONVERTIBLE CURRENCIES[1]

$m.

End of Year	Germany	France	Italy[2]	Netherlands	BLEU[3]	EEC	UK	USA
1958	4412	1050	2139	1246	1345	10192	3069	20582
1962	6439	3610	3619	1743	1622	17033	2806	16156
1963	7098	4457	3181	1899	1802	18437	2657	15808
1964	6969	5105	3678	2084	1992	19828	2316	15903
1965	6353	5459	3867	2058	1996	19732	3004	14587
1966	6771	5745	3702	2036	1952	20206	3100	14556
1967								

[1] Central Banks' gross reserves plus those of the *Fonds de stabilisation des changes* in France, of the *Ufficio Italiano Cambi* in Italy, and of the Treasury in the United States, Reserves of the United Kingdom Exchange Equalization Account.

[2] Revised Series; including foreign exchange held by the *Banca d'Italia* on behalf of the *Ufficio Italiano Cambi* as a '*banca abilitata*'.

[3] *Banque Nationale de Belgique.*

TABLE E: THE FLOW OF FINANCIAL RESOURCES
TO LESS DEVELOPED COUNTRIES AND MULTILATERAL AGENCIES

(i) The Flow of Official Financial Resources

(Million US dollars)

	Germany	France	Italy	Netherlands	Belgium	EEC	UK	US	DAC[1]
1956	161	647	43	48	20	919	205	2006	(3312)
1957	297	819	164	23	20	1323	234	2091	(3859)
1958	278	884	73	40	23	1298	276	2410	(4419)
1959	325	835	84	49	79	1372	377	2322	(4398)
1960	343	848	110	47	101	1449	407	2834	4989
1961	615	943	85	69	92	1804	457	3530	6107
1962	450	977	110	91	80	1708	421	3671	6114
1963	424	851	110	38	92	1515	415	3755	6125
1964	423	831	54	48	84	1440	493	3463	5883
1965	427	757	66	60	121	1431	480	3766	6281
1966									
1967									

( ) Preliminary figures or OECD Secretariat estimate. [1] Development Assistance Committee, consisting of all members of the organization for Economic Co-operation and Development and, in addition, Japan.

(ii) *The Net Flow of Private Capital*

(Million US dollars)

	Germany	France	Italy	Netherlands	Belgium	EEC	UK	US	DAC
1956	275	477	91	232	70	1145	384	1230	(2881)
1957	248	408	45	124	16	841	723	2009	(3692)
1958	242	453	82	160	89	1026	392	1275	(2822)
1959	474	337	65	215	89	1180	467	954	(2698)
1960	274	477	193	203	81	1228	389	1042	2958
1961	219	489	177	144	82	1131	444	1099	3061
1962	182	431	302	52	48	1015	306	819	2450
1963	165	414	233	109	95	1016	280	880	2390
1964	268	550	188	80	93	1179	415	1297	3200
1965	278	562	184	164	120	1308	443	(1748)	3870
1966									
1967									

( ) Preliminary figures or OECD Secretariat estimate.

(iii) The Total Official and Private Flow

(Million US Dollars)

	Germany	France	Italy	Netherlands	Belgium	EEC	UK	US	DAC
1956	436	1124	134	280	90	2064	589	3236	(6193)
1957	545	1227	209	147	36	2164	957	4100	(7551)
1958	520	1337	155	200	112	2324	668	3685	(7241)
1959	799	1172	149	264	168	2492	844	3276	(7096)
1960	616	1325	303	250	182	2676	796	3876	7947
1961	835	1432	262	214	175	2918	901	4629	9167
1962	632	1408	412	143	128	2623	727	4490	8564
1963	589	1265	343	147	187	2531	695	4634	8515
1964	691	1382	242	128	177	2620	908	4760	9083
1965	705	1319	250	224	241	2739	923	5514	10150
1966									
1967									

( ) Preliminary figures or OECD Secretariat estimate.
Source: OECD. *Development Assistance Efforts and Policies 1966 Review.*

DOCUMENT 10. THE WORKING OF THE INSTITUTIONS. (A LECTURE ORIGINALLY GIVEN TO THE CONSERVATIVE POLITICAL CENTRE SUMMER SCHOOL IN 1962 BY M. EMILE NOËL, THE EXECUTIVE SECRETARY OF THE EEC COMMISSION, AND RE-WRITTEN BY HIM FOR THIS BOOK TO TAKE ACCOUNT OF DEVELOPMENTS UP TO MARCH 1966.)

It is difficult to say to what order the institutional system of the Community belongs. The Community is much more than an intergovernmental organization. Its institutions have their own personality and extensive powers. Nor does the Community form a 'federal government' to which, in its spheres of competence, the national Governments and Parliaments might in some way be subordinated. In fact, we in Brussels have refrained from putting our institutional system into any one of the categories defined by experts on international law, leaving this task to future historians. And if we are asked to define in one word the institutional system of the Communities, we prefer to say simply that it is a 'Community' system.

THE INSTITUTIONS

The Rome Treaty lays down that the tasks entrusted to the Community shall be carried out by four Institutions: the European Parliament, the Council of Ministers, the Commission and the Court of Justice.

The Parliament consists of 142 members appointed by the six national Parliaments from among their own members.

The Council consists of the representatives of the Member States, each Government delegating one of its Ministers to attend meetings. The composition of the Council may thus vary according to the subjects on the agenda. Though the Foreign Minister is to some extent regarded as his country's chief representative on the Council, the Ministers of Agriculture, of Transport, of Finance, etc., often take part in meetings, either alone or accompanying the Minister for Foreign Affairs.

The Commission consists of nine members appointed for four years by unanimous agreement between the six Governments. During the whole of their period of office, the members of the Commission must act in complete independence both of their Governments and of the Council of Ministers. The Council has no power to terminate the mandate of a member of the Commission. Only the Parliament could procure the automatic resignation of the Commission by passing a vote of no confidence.

The Council and the Commission are assisted by the Economic and Social Committee, a consultative body composed of representatives of the various walks of life, industry, farming, trade unions, etc. In many matters the Council and the Commission must consult the Committee before they can take a formal decision. The Committee also ensures that professional and business circles play their part in the development of the Community.

Lastly, the Court of Justice, consisting of seven judges appointed for six years by agreement between the Governments, ensures that in the implementation of the Treaty the law is duly observed.

I should like to supplement this brief description of the institutions with a word on the formal steps which the Council and the Commission can take in execution of the tasks entrusted to them.

First, they can adopt Regulations. Under the Treaty, the Regulation has a general application; it is binding in every respect and directly applicable in each Member State.

They can also issue Directives to one or more of the Member States. A Directive shall bind any Member State to which it is addressed, as to the result to be achieved, while leaving it to the authorities of that State to decide on the form and the means to be employed.

They can take Decisions, to be addressed either to a government, a firm or an individual. A decision shall be binding in all its parts on those to whom it is addressed.

Lastly, they can formulate Recommendations or Opinions, which have no binding force.

I shall have to go rather more fully into the internal functioning of the Commission and the Council and the way in which relations between the Commission and the Council on the one hand and between the Commission and the European Parliament on the other are organized. Commission and Council provide and transmit the driving force which keeps the entire institutional system of the Communities moving forward, and the way they are geared together is perhaps the most original aspect of the system. At the same time the importance and the political authority of the Commission, without which it could not play its full role vis-à-vis the Council, stem from the fact that the Commission is responsible to the Parliament alone.

The Treaty gives the Commission extensive responsibilities which can best be outlined as follows:

The Commission is the guardian of the Treaty. The Commission is the executive organ of the Community. The Commission initiates Community policy and gives expression to the Community aspect of matters discussed in the Council.

First of all, the Commission is the guardian of the Treaty.

The Commission sees to it that the Treaty's provisions and the decisions taken by the Institutions are correctly applied. It is responsible for maintaining an atmosphere of mutual confidence. If the Commission does its job of 'watchdog' properly, everyone can fulfil his obligations without mental reservation, knowing that his partners are doing the same and that action will be taken against any breach of the Treaty. Conversely, nobody can plead any shortcoming of his partners as an excuse for not fulfilling his own obligations. If there are any shortcomings, it is up to the Commission as an impartial body to make inquiries, to give an objective judgement and to prescribe what measures the State at fault must take to right the situation.

The Treaty lays down a strict procedure for putting a stop to breaches. If the Commission considers that there has been any such breach—and it can reach this conclusion either as a result of *ex officio* inquiry, or at the request of a Government, or by investigating complaints from private persons—it can call on the State concerned to submit its comments or justify its action within a specified period (a month or six weeks). If the Member State continues the practice in question and if its comments do not induce the Commission to modify its view, the Commission issues a reasoned Opinion (an *avis motivé*), with which the Member State is obliged to comply within the time-limit prescribed by the Commission. If the Member State does not do so, the Commission may put the case to the Court of Justice, whose decision is binding both on the Member State and on the Institutions.

These provisions, which give considerable power to the Institutions, are in fact fully applied. In 1964, for example, the Commission dealt with 24 alleged infringements, investigation of which gave the following results:

In ten cases the State concerned took the necessary corrective action forthwith, i.e. as soon as the Commission asked for comments. In three other, very complex, cases the comments of the State concerned led the Commission to look further into the matter, and the Commission has not so far taken the proceedings further.

In the eleven other cases the Commission issued a reasoned opinion. In four of these the States concerned have acted in conformity with this opinion.

In a fifth instance—a more complex one—a means of solving the special problems of the State concerned, which led to the adoption of a solution out of line with the Treaty, will shortly be provided through the adoption of Community rules in the matter.

The remaining six cases were referred by the Commission to the Court of Justice, which subsequently suspended proceedings in one of them as the State involved had meanwhile taken the action called for. The Court has handed down three decisions which have very largely upheld the Commission's viewpoint. Two cases are still pending.

In addition, nearly seventy-five files on suspected breaches were before the Commission at the end of 1964 and were dealt with during 1965.

These figures are large in comparison with the fifty cases brought during the first five years of the Community's existence, from 1958 to the end of 1962. This is because the provisions of the Treaty become more stringent as the stages of its implementation progress, while the extension of Community legislation multiplies opportunities for mistakes. Most of the cases during the early years were concerned with customs duties and quotas. Now there are as many which concern the application of the agricultural regulations. The variety of subject matter is likely to increase in the future as other common policies come into force. The Commission's 'policing' activities are therefore very unlikely to become fewer.

Be this as it may, the measures that have given rise to these proceedings have been of very limited economic significance. As a general rule there has been no question of deliberate action to escape obligations under the Treaty, but of differences of interpretation between the Commission and a Member State, on which the Court has decided, or of errors which are almost inevitable when national administrations must adapt themselves to the relevant Community procedures. It would be fair to say that the breaches committed so far have had no great effect on the correct implementation of the provisions laid down in the Treaty.

The Commission is the executive organ of the Community

Considerable executive powers are already vested in the Commission, and they will increase in the future.

The Commission has its own power of decision. Both the Treaty and Regulations made under it entrust the Commission with the task of drawing up texts (we might call them 'administrative decrees') which give effect to the 'European laws' contained in the Treaty or adopted by the Council, and accord it the necessary powers. As the Council has made great use, particularly in the implementation of the common agricultural policy, of the authority vested in it by the Treaty to confer such executive powers on the Commission, the number of decisions or regulations issued by the latter has increased considerably since 1962.

Thus, between 1958 and 1 July 1962 (when the first agricultural market organizations began to function) a total of 55 regulations came into force, of which only nine were Commission regulations. In the three months between 1 July and 1 October 1962 the establishment of the first agricultural market organizations (cereals, livestock products, fruit and vegetables) led the Commission alone to adopt 70 implementing regulations. To give another example, in 1964 the Commission adopted a total of 124 regulations almost all connected with the administration of the market organizations set up in 1962 and with the establishment of three further organizations (for milk or milk products, beef and veal, and rice).

89

The Commission must also take most of the individual decisions required by the Treaty or the regulations pursuant to it. These decisions may be addressed to a Government in order, for example, to grant or to refuse tariff quotas, or to adjust or prohibit a State aid, or to authorize some departure from the Treaty under the safeguard clauses. They may also be aimed directly at a firm or individual: the Regulation on monopolies and restrictive practices gives the Commission exclusive power to authorize 'good agreements'.

The Commission also has direct supervisory powers. For instance, in matters of restrictive practices or transport rates it can on behalf of the Community institute on-the-spot inquiries in the firms themselves, take samples or make checks.

In the early days of the Community the Commission had relatively few occasions to take decisions of its own. Between 1958 and July 1962 they totalled no more than 200—and the bulk of them concerned tariff quotas.

In this field too the agricultural regulations and the regulations on cartels have considerably swollen the Commission's work. The Commission must for instance take decisions at regular intervals, and sometimes even from day to day, on the basis to be used for calculating the levies on cereals, rice and dairy products. In 1964 alone, the Commission had to issue a total of 205 decisions in addition to the almost daily decisions and the administration of the tariff quotas which between them had previously formed the bulk of the questions it had to settle.

By 30 September 1965, 78 proceedings in the cartel field, covering a total of 240 particular cases (some of them now settled) had been initiated by the Commission.

The Commission's financial management tasks are also considerable. From the beginning it has had to administer the European Social Fund (£8 million for 1966) for the retraining or resettlement of unemployed workers. It also administers the European Development Fund, renewed in 1964 by the Yaoundé Convention, which associates the African States and Madagascar with the Community, and has at its disposal £286 million for five years.

Even larger sums are to be allocated in the future to the European Agricultural Guidance and Guarantee Fund, also administered by the Commission. An amount of £107 for this Fund figures in the 1966 budget. In a few years, when free movement for farm products is an established fact, the Fund will have at its disposal more than £540 million each year, which will be used to enable the Community to take over the cost of supporting the agricultural markets in each Member State and—one quarter of the total sum—to grant Community help for improving the structure of agriculture.

THE MANAGEMENT COMMITTEES

We have already noted that it was the Council which, by vesting further executive powers in the Commission, made possible this considerable extension of the latter's management activities. In a great number of cases the Council wished to be sure that these powers would be exercised in close liaison with the Member Governments. This led to the establishment with the Commission of various committees of Government representatives. Some of these are purely advisory, but the most original arrangement and the one which has proved most fruitful in practice is the 'Management Committee'.

Originally, the Management Committees were a component of the agricultural market organization. One such Committee was to operate for each main category of products. In view of the success of these Committees, the arrangement was later adopted in other sectors of Community activity.

The procedure is as follows: the implementing measure to be taken by the Commission is submitted as a draft to the competent Management Committee, which gives an opinion on it (the votes of members are weighted as in the Council).

The Committee's opinion is not binding on the Commission, which after studying it has complete freedom of decision, the measure it decides on being immediately enforceable. However, if the opinion has been given by qualified majority (12 votes out of 17) and if the Commission does not accept it, the matter is referred to the Council, which then has one month within which it may amend the Commission's decision. If, on the other hand, the Commission decision conforms with the Committee's opinion or if the Committee, for lack of a qualified majority for any particular view, has failed to give an opinion, the Commission's decision is final and there is no appeal against it to the Council.

Experience has shown that the Management Committee procedure is fully satisfactory. Between July 1962 and March 1965, for instance, there were about 200 meetings of the various Management Committees. Following their discussions, 350 Commission regulations or decisions were adopted. It is even more interesting to note that only three of these measures were referred to the Council, which amended only one.

This gives an idea of the atmosphere of co-operation and confidence that has grown up in the Management Committee between the Commission's staff and the officials of the several administrations which subsequently have to apply the measures enacted by the Commission.

A simple parallel will serve to illustrate the role of the Management Committees: they are in a way a sort of alarm system. When the Commission deviates from an opinion given by qualified majority, i.e. with the approval of the bulk of the representatives of Member States, this is a sign that a difficult situation or a serious problem exists. It is then only reasonable that the Council itself should be able to discuss the matter. The fact that this procedure is scarcely used bears witness to the effectiveness of the system and the excellent understanding among all concerned.

The Commission initiates policy and maintains its unity and coherence

Initiation of Community policy and representation of the Community interest are no doubt the Commission's most important and perhaps most original tasks. The Commission acts in close co-operation with the Council, so that if I describe this aspect of the Commission's activities to you I will at the same time be explaining the greater part of what the Council has to do and how it does it.

The Common Market Treaty is frequently defined as an outline treaty—*un traité-cadre*—as distinct from the Euratom Treaty and the Coal and Steel Treaty, which may be called 'law-establishing treaties'—*des traités-lois*. Whereas these two Treaties specify exhaustively the rules to be applied within relatively narrow sectors, the Treaty establishing the Common Market (apart from its 'automatic' clauses on customs and the dismantling of quotas) confines itself to indicating the general lines of policy to be followed by the Community, in the main spheres of economic activity, leaving it to the Institutions—and particularly the Council and the Commission in co-operation with the Parliament—to elaborate the provisions that will be applied in the Community.

In a way, everything connected with the economic union was left blank in the Treaty, but these blanks can be filled in by the Community's Institutions without any new treaties being concluded or new parliamentary ratification being obtained. The measures that the Institutions are empowered to take are real 'European laws' that can be directly applied in all Member States and may bring about far-reaching changes in the branches of the economy they concern. The European laws on agriculture adopted by the Council since the beginning of 1962 form a whole of a significance at least comparable to that of the entire Coal and Steel Treaty.

Let me just touch upon a comment that is often made—that the Common Market Treaty is less 'supranational', more intergovernmental than the Coal and Steel Treaty. In my opinion, this is really an optical illusion. The Coal and Steel Treaty laid down in full detail the implementing powers entrusted to the High Authority. On the other hand, we shall have to wait for the common policies to be framed before we know what powers of implementation the Common Market Commission will have in all the spheres covered by the Rome Treaty. We know this already as far as restrictive practices and agriculture are concerned, and everyone can see that these powers are as extensive as those of the High Authority.

The Treaty of Paris and the Treaty of Rome are based on similar principles and set up comparable institutional systems. But as the Common Market is in process of continuous creation and leaves scope for solutions to be found pragmatically and adapted to a given sector or a given situation, the Treaty of Rome has perhaps been less alarming even to those people who have most reservations with respect to the establishment of the Community, and at the same time it makes the balance between the powers of national Governments and those of the European Institutions more evident to those who are just beginning to accept the Communities. The difficulties the

Common Market experienced in 1965 in no way invalidate this view.

These considerations can help us to a fuller understanding of the role of the Institutions in putting the Treaty into effect. First of all, they have to create out of nothing the structure of economic union in Europe. The Treaty provides the foundations, but the house itself has still to be built. Once the structure is there, the institutions will also have to frame Community policy and apply it from day to day. To guide the whole of this process the Treaty makes the Commission today the architect of the new building and tomorrow the initiator of the common policy.

All provisions of a general scope or of a certain degree of importance must in fact be passed by the Council of Ministers, but—with a few specific exceptions—the Council can only come to a decision on a proposal of the Commission; it is therefore always for the Commission to take the initiative. If the Commission does not submit any proposals, the Council is paralysed and the Community's progress halted. This is equally true in agriculture, transport, commercial policy, or approximation of legislation.

In order to give an idea of the dimensions of these activities, it may be pointed out that in 1964, for instance, the Commission sent to the Council 156 proposals and 96 other communications of various sorts. In the same year the Council adopted, on proposals from the Commission, 80 regulations, 14 directives, 55 decisions and an important recommendation on the fight against inflation.

The submission of a proposal initiates the dialogue between the Ministers in the Council (who express the points of view of the various countries) and the Commission—a 'European' body that is called upon to express the interest of the Community as a whole and to seek 'European' solutions to common problems. It might be feared that this dialogue could be distorted if the Commission were in too weak a position *vis-à-vis* the Governments—strong in their authority and the attributes of sovereignty. The Treaty balances the situation quite ingeniously.

By the very fact of formulating the proposal on the basis of which the Council is to hold its discussion (and it is only on this basis that the Council can discuss) the Commission already acquires real influence. But there is more to it than this.

Article 149 of the Treaty, which is perhaps one of the keys to our institutional system, stipulates: 'When, pursuant to the Treaty, the Council acts on a proposal of the Commission, it shall, where the amendment of such proposal is involved, act only by means of a unanimous vote.'

Provided it is unanimous, the Council of Ministers can therefore take a sovereign decision even against the Commission's proposal. And this is only reasonable, since the Council then expresses the common standpoint of all member Governments.

Conversely, a decision may be taken by a majority only if it is in conformity with the Commission's proposal. In other words, if the Member States are not agreed, they can take their decision by a majority only by accepting the Commission's proposal, which they have no power to change. In such a case only the Commission itself can amend its proposal. Where the majority rule can operate, then, the situation is the following: either the Council adopts the Commission proposal as it stands by majority vote, or it takes a different decision unanimously, or it is unable to take any decision. This means that the Commission has a genuine negotiating power in the Council. Discussion can be joined and it is in fact joined on the ground chosen by the European body.

This dialogue has a momentum of its own. The application of the majority rule—this we know from long experience in the Community—does not mean riding rough-shod over a minority. When working out its proposal the Commission will have taken into consideration the often widely different interests of the Member States and endeavoured to bring out the general interest. As is normal in such a small 'club', both the members of the Council and the Commission have a preference for agreeing on a joint position. The possibility of a decision being taken by majority vote can, therefore, prompt a member to abandon an extreme or isolated position, while the concern for harmony may encourage the Commission and those members of the Council who have accepted its proposal

95

to make the necessary efforts to bring about a *rapprochement*. In this way—and practice has confirmed this rather paradoxical conclusion—the majority rule makes unanimous adoption of proposals much easier and speedier. In this subtle game the Commission always has a determining role.

Thus the Commission occupies a central position in the Council, where it can permanently play the role of honest broker, of mediator between Governments, at the same time as it supplies the drive and exerts the pressure needed to reach agreed formulae.

The political consequences are still more important. Proposals from the Commission are the expression of a policy it has framed with no other consideration in mind than the common interest of the Community as a whole. The permanent status of the Commission during its four years in office ensures the continuity of this policy, and the Council can only decide on texts submitted by the Commission, which are the means of putting the policy into effect. It is therefore not possible for the Council to adopt contradictory proposals on different subjects —by means of changing majorities or at the whim of pressure groups or struggles for influence between Governments. It is also impossible for a majority on the Council without the consent of the Commission to impose on a State in the minority any measure that would gravely harm its vital interests. If the Commission really fulfils its obligations, it cannot be party to such an action. Its intervention is therefore an important guarantee to the 'small States' in particular, and these have always set great store by it.

UNANIMITY AND MAJORITY

During the first two stages of the transitional period unanimity was required for most Council decisions, so that the procedure described above applied to only a relatively limited number of matters. The Community spirit of the Council members and also the authority of the Commission and the personal standing of its individual members nevertheless ensured that the discussion was conducted in a satisfactory manner in all cases and that the Commission was fully able to play its part as moving spirit and as conciliator.

At a time when the transition to the third stage, on 1 January 1966, would have permitted a considerable widening of the possibilities for majority decisions, the application of the majority rule became the crux of a crisis in the Community. Was it really possible, contended one Government, that a Member State should be placed in a minority when one of its vital interests was at stake?

It is not possible to answer such a question simply by referring to the texts, any more than it is possible to give an objective definition of a 'vital interest'. Furthermore, if we limit ourselves to thinking in terms of interests, it is by no means impossible that, in matters where each Member State has renounced its freedom of action in favour of the Community, a veto on a Community decision in the name of a national interest would infringe some vital interests of other Member States, which are harmed through the paralysis of the Community. On the other hand those who accept the Community system and have confidence in its internal logic, its institutions, their rules and their traditions, can find in them every guarantee that can reasonably be sought.

The general interest of the Community must of necessity take account of any vital interest of one of its members. The institutions therefore have a duty to take any such interest into full consideration. Moreover the close union of peoples which the Community is intended to establish would not be possible if any one of its peoples were gravely injured in its vital interests. Finally, the system of discussion in the Council which we have just described is conducive to the widest possible agreement. From the opposite standpoint, even when there is unanimity, no member of a Community can ignore the general interest when deciding what constitutes his own interest: unanimity in a Community cannot be equated with an unconditional right of veto.

Thus in a living Community any abuse of majority voting (and this would probably be equally true of the abuse of unanimity) is a theoretical risk which the constant strengthening of internal links due to the very development of the Community makes increasingly unlikely, whereas the possibility of majority decisions gives flexibility and drive to the whole system.

Confidence in the future, in the will to agree and in the

wisdom of the institutions and Governments, is therefore the only possible answer. And is not this the real meaning of the conclusions reached on 21 January 1966 in Luxembourg when the Council—the six Ministers of Foreign Affairs—recognized that the absence of agreement between them on how the majority rule should be applied was no obstacle to their further work in common?

RELATIONS BETWEEN PARLIAMENT AND COMMISSION

For the dialogue between Commission and Council to be genuine, it is also necessary for the independence of the Commission to be guaranteed. To this end, as I pointed out earlier, the Treaty stipulates that the Commission shall be responsible to the European Parliament and to that Parliament alone. The composition of the Parliament makes it essentially a Community body, completely integrated. There are no national divisions, but only political groups organized at European level. The Parliament exercises permanent control over the Commission, making sure that it respects its role as representative of the Community interest, and always prepared to call it to order should there be any reason to suspect that it is yielding to canvassing by one or more of the Governments. Furthermore, the Parliament must be expressly consulted on the Commission's main proposals before the Council takes any decision.

The parliamentary committees play an important part in this field. The Parliament can hardly hold more than six or seven sessions per year, each lasting a week. Between these sessions, most of the parliamentary committees meet once or even more often. Whatever subject it is dealing with, a parliamentary committee invites the responsible member of the Executive to explain his standpoint—whether on decisions taken by the Executive, on proposals submitted to the Council or on the attitude adopted by the Executive in the Council.

The committees deal with matters in detail, and as their meetings are held in private they can be given fuller and even confidential information. Their work, which I think is considerably different in nature from that of the committees of the British Parliament, has contributed much to extending the influence of the European Parliament on current affairs.

The written questions that the members of the European Parliament can put to the Commission (and to the Council of Ministers) are also a means of parliamentary control that is being used more and more. During the parliamentary year 1964-5, 95 written questions were put to the Common Market Commission.

The widening of the Community's responsibilities will later make it necessary for the powers of the European Parliament to be widened also, and for its representative character to be strengthened—for instance through election by direct universal suffrage. We in Brussels are convinced that such a development is inevitable, whatever opposition may have held it up so far.

Parliamentary control thus ensures the independence of the Commission, thanks to which the Council enjoys the advantages of majority voting while being preserved   as far as is possible —from its few attendant risks.

METHODS OF WORK

Now that I have analysed the main tasks of the Institutions, the nature of their relations and the way in which their powers are balanced, I should like to give you some indication of how work is actually done in the Community.

How does the Commission function?

The Commission's staff is divided into nine Directorates-General, an Executive Secretariat (which has a co-ordinating role) and the Spokesman's Group. There are also three 'services'—legal, statistical and information—which are common to the three Communities. The total staff of the Commission at present numbers about 3,300, almost 900 of whom are officials in positions of responsibility (what we call grade A), and a large linguistic service. Together with the staff of the Parliament, the Council and the Court of Justice, the total employed by the Common Market is more than 4,000 people. In the 1966 budget the operational expenses of the staff serving the Commission and the three other Institutions (Common Market share) amounted to £14 million.

Within the Commission itself, each of its nine Members has special responsibility for one of the main spheres of Community activity (external relations, agriculture, social affairs, etc.) and has the corresponding Directorate-General under his authority.

The Treaty lays down, however, that the Commission must act as a collegiate body with cabinet responsibility. In other words, all the acts that the Treaty or its implementing regulations entrust explicitly to the Commission (Regulations, Decisions, proposals to the Council, etc.) must be performed by the Commission as a whole. The Commission cannot therefore delegate to one of its Members powers in the sphere of his special responsibility that would give him a degree of independence comparable, say, with that of a Minister in his own department.

In order that this collegiate system should not constitute such a burden of work that it would paralyse the Commission, frequent use is made of what we call in our own jargon the 'written procedure'. The members of the Commission receive the dossier and a draft decision concerning a matter under discussion; if they have not submitted reservations or objections within a fixed period (generally a week), the proposal is deemed to have been adopted. To give you an idea of how this works out, I may tell you that in this way more than 1,700 decisions of all kinds were reached in the course of 1964. Consequently, it is only questions of some importance that appear on the agenda for Commission meetings, which take up one whole day every week.

For the most delicate questions the members of the Commission meet alone, no official being present except the Executive Secretary and the Deputy Executive Secretary. For routine matters—or those of a technical nature—the responsible officials can be called in. Although Commission decisions can be taken by a majority vote, most of them are unanimous. The solidarity of the members of the Commission and the underlying unity of their views, which transcend differences in character and background, make quite a considerable impression on anyone who has the opportunity of following the activities of this body. It is in fact rather rare for matters to be put to the vote in the Commission, and when this has happened the minority has always considered itself bound by the majority decision.

ELABORATION OF THE COMMISSION'S DECISIONS AND PROPOSALS
TO THE COUNCIL

In connection with the Commission's own Decisions and with the proposals it submits to the Council, two very different cases must be distinguished: first, defining the main lines of the policy the Commission intends to follow in a given sphere, and secondly, elaboration of the ways and means of putting such a policy into practice or of measures of a technical rather than a political nature.

When the Commission has to lay down the main lines of policy, it first enters into consultations on the broadest possible basis, seeking the opinions of Governments, public officials and private organizations, after which it takes its decisions with the assistance of its own staff but of no one else. This it does at working meetings which are often numerous and lengthy, with weeks of reflection between them. The method was used to prepare documents as important as the Commission's first memorandum on European problems after the breakdown of the Free Trade Area negotiations, the proposal to speed up the implementation of the Treaty, the memoranda on the common agricultural policy and on the transport policy, the proposals on the renewal of the Convention of Association with the African States and Madagascar, the proposals on a common cereals price level, etc.

On the other hand, when the Commission has to decide on the broad lines and settle the ways and means of a decision with a definite political importance, it regularly calls on technical experts from the six member countries. In such a case the departments concerned convene and preside over meetings of government experts appointed by each of the national administrations concerned. These experts do not formally commit their administrations, but as they are adequately informed of the latter's interests and opinions, they perform a useful function in guiding the Commission in its search for solutions that are technically in order and generally acceptable to the six Governments.

These meetings of experts are held very frequently. In 1964, for instance, about 1,300 meetings of this kind were organized by the Commission on the most varied subjects connected with the implementation of the Treaty. From year to year this provides an increasing number of civil servants from the various countries with a truly European education.

These meetings also enable contact to be made at the administrative level between European officials and Government officials. They are supplemented by many consultative meetings that the members or officials of the Commission organize with leaders of the trade unions, of employers' associations, farmers' unions, dealers' associations, etc., of the Six, which have established groups to represent them at Community level. Some of these Committees are on a permanent footing. Thus the Council, acting on a proposal from the Commission, has set up the Short-term Economic Policy Committee, the Budget Policy Committee and the Committee for Medium-term Economic Policy, all composed of senior Government representatives. The committees dealing with occupational training and the free movement of workers are mixed (Government experts and delegates from industrial and trade organizations). Finally, the Commission itself has set up several advisory committees, such as those for the main classes of agricultural produce or for the study of certain social problems, which consist of the leaders of all the trade organizations concerned.

The results of all this preparatory work are ultimately laid before the Commission, which has to take the final decision. This, then, is how proposals submitted to the Council by the Commission are drawn up—and also, very often, Regulations or Decisions that the Commission itself can adopt but in the preparation of which it endeavours to ensure that the national administrations have their say.

How does the Council work?

When the Council has before it a Commission memorandum of general scope or a proposal on a well-defined subject, it entrusts the preparation of its discussions either to an *ad hoc* committee of senior officials (such as the Special Committee for Agriculture) or to one of its permanent working parties (of which there is one for each main branch of the Community's activities). The work of these bodies is co-ordinated by the Committee of

Permanent Representatives, a committee of Ambassadors which prepares the work of the Council.

The Commission is represented at all meetings of working parties, of special committees, and of the Committee of Permanent Representatives, so that the dialogue that began with experts from the various countries can be carried further with officials duly appointed by their Governments.

Council decisions may only be taken by the Ministers themselves, though on less important questions and where unanimous agreement has been reached between the six Permanent Representatives and the Representatives of the Commission, the decision is taken by the Council without discussion.

On the other hand, all questions of any importance or of political significance are thoroughly discussed in the Council by the Ministers and the members of the Commission, who take part in the Council meetings as of right.

It is at this point that the rules of Article 149, which I have described above, come into play.

These meetings are not a pure formality, as is sometimes the case with ministerial meetings in other international organizations, but working meetings at which discussion is often prolonged and fierce and the final result long uncertain. Sessions of the Council are moreover very frequent and often long. In 1964, for example, the Council held 36 sessions lasting between them for 67 days. When a decision is near on a particularly thorny problem, the Council may settle down to a 'marathon session'. Everybody in the Community will remember the session on the agricultural regulations at the turn of the year 1961–2, which went on for nearly three weeks. And this has not been the only one!

These then are the rules and the procedures that seem to me most typical for the functioning of the Common Market's Council of Ministers and Commission and—more generally— for the Community as a whole. If I had to go on and describe the *style* of our institutions in Brussels, I would do no more than make these three observations:

First the institutions, and particularly the Commission, are not inward-looking. On the contrary, they are focal points for the constant interchange of opinions and suggestions of Governments and civil servants, of European parliamentarians, and of representatives of labour and management. Secondly, there are strict legal rules that must be rigorously respected, but at the same time the maintenance of permanent contacts creates that common spirit and mutual confidence which ensure the necessary flexibility. Finally trade organizations, parliamentary circles, the civil servants of the various countries and also their Ministers have real confidence in the impartiality of the Commission.

After eight years' development of the Common Market, after the even longer experience of the European Coal and Steel Community, after several crises weathered—of which the most recent was also the most serious—it would seem that the efficacy of the Community system, the strength of its institutions and the roots they have taken among the peoples of the Community are proven beyond doubt. True, the pace at which the Community advances has always depended on the will of the Governments and of the peoples composing it. However, as long as respect for the Treaty remains a common foundation of the policy of the Member States, we may rest assured that there will be no difficulties, however great, which it will not in the last resort be possible to resolve, as we move forward to the complete establishment of the European Communities.

DOCUMENT II. EXTRACTS FROM THE DRAFT CONVENTION ADOPTED BY THE EUROPEAN PARLIAMENT ON 17 MAY 1960

The Council of Ministers of the European Coal and Steel Community,
The Council of the European Economic Community,
The Council of the European Atomic Energy Community,
— being resolved to base the mission entrusted to the European Parliament on the freely expressed will of the peoples of the member states of the European Communities,
— wishing to increase the representative character of the European Parliament,
— in the light of Article 21 of the Treaty establishing ECSC,
— in the light of Article 138 of the Treaty establishing EEC,

— in the light of Article 108 of the Treaty establishing Euratom,

— in the light of the draft prepared by the European Parliament and adopted by it on 17 May 1960,

hereby draw up the following provisions, whose adoption has been recommended to the Member States.

Chapter 1 Concerning the Elected Assembly

Article 1. The representatives of the peoples to the European Parliament are elected by direct universal suffrage.

Article 2. The number of representatives elected in each Member State is fixed as follows:

Belgium	–	–	–	–	42
France	–	–	–	–	108
Germany (Fed. Rep.)	–	–	108
Italy –	–	–	–	–	108
Luxembourg –	–	–	–	18
Netherlands –	–	–	–	42

Article 3. During a transition period a third of these representatives are elected by the parliaments from among their own membership according to a procedure which ensures the equitable representation of the political groups.

Article 4. The transition period begins on the date on which the present convention comes into force.

Its length shall be fixed by the European Parliament. It may not end before the close of the third state of the establishment of the Common Market, as defined in Article 8 of the Treaty establishing EEC; it may not end later than the dissolution of the legislature (*législature*) during which the third stage comes to an end.

Article 5. (1) The representatives are elected for five years.

However, the mandate of the representatives elected by the parliaments shall end with loss of mandate in a national parliament or at the end of the period for which the representatives have been elected by their national parliaments. Any representative whose mandate ends in this way retains his office until his successor has been accepted as a member of the European Parliament.

(2) The five-year legislative period starts with the opening of the first session held after each election.

Article 6. The representatives shall vote individually and personally. They may receive neither instructions nor an imperative mandate.

Article 7. During the transition period membership of the Parliament is compatible with membership of a national parliament.

The Assembly shall decide on the compatibility of these mandates after the close of the transition period.

Article 8. (1) During the transition period,
  (*a*) Membership of the Parliament is incompatible with:

— membership of the government of a Member State,
— membership of the High Authority of ECSC, of the Commission of EEC or of the Euratom Commission,
— the post of judge, advocate-general or clerk to the Court of Justice of the European Communities,
— membership of the Consultative Committee of ECSC or of the Economic and Social Committee of EEC and Euratom . . .

The representatives of the European Parliament who, during the life of a legislature are appointed to one of these functions, are to be replaced under the terms of Article 17.

  (*b*) Each Member State shall determine whether, and to what extent, the incompatibilities defined by its national laws for membership of the national parliament shall apply to membership of the European Parliament.

(2) The Parliament will decide on the system of incompatibilities to be applied after the end of the transition period.

Chapter 11 Concerning the Electoral System

Article 9. The European Parliament shall draw up the provisions which will govern the election of representatives, according to a procedure that shall be as uniform as possible, after the close of the transition period provided for in Article 4.

Until these provisions apply, the electoral system will remain within the competence of each Member State, subject to the terms of the present Convention.

Article 10. The electorate shall consist, within each Member State, subject to the provisions of Article 11 of those men and women who meet the qualifications within each Member State for participating in elections by direct universal suffrage for the national parliament.

Article 11. The age qualification for voting may not be less than twenty-one years.

Nationals of a Member State living in another Member State shall have the right to exercise their vote in their countries of origin, which shall take the necessary steps for this end.

In the case of the state where they are residing also allowing these persons the right to vote, they may only vote once. Any infringement of this rule shall be subject to the penalties laid down in the laws of the voter's country of origin.

Article 12. In each Member State every man or woman, who is over twenty-five years old and a citizen of one of the member states may stand for election, subject to any traditional ineligibility imposed by national law.

The incompatibilities laid down in Article 8 do not entail ineligibility for election.

Article 13. The constitutional provisions which cover the admission of political parties to elections in each member state shall apply to the election of the European Parliament.

Article 14. The elections for the European Parliament shall be held on the same day in all six Member States: the date shall be fixed in such a way that national elections do not coincide with those for the European Parliament.

However, for either traditional reasons or geographical conditions, any Member State may decide to hold the elections on the eve of the appointed day or on the day following it, or to spread them over all three days.

Article 15. (1) The election of the European Parliament shall be held at the latest one month before the end of each legislature.

(2) The European Parliament shall meet, as of right, on the first Tuesday after the expiration of one month from the date of the election.

(3) The outgoing Parliament shall remain in office until the first meeting of the new Assembly.

Article 16. The European Parliament shall verify the credentials of the representatives and rule on any disputes which may arise concerning this.

Article 17. In the event of a seat filled by universal suffrage falling vacant, a by-election shall not be held.

During the transition period, national law must establish electoral provisions which will permit, subject to this condition, the seat to be filled by a new member.

In the case of a vacancy arising, under Article 3, the Parliament of the member state shall elect or appoint a successor to it.

Article 18. Those candidates or lists obtaining a minimum of 10 per cent of the votes cast in the constituency where they stand shall be entitled to the repayment of certain electoral expenses.

The necessary credits will be provided in the budget of the European Parliament in order to permit this reimbursement according to the procedure fixed in advance by the Bureau of the Assembly . . .

DOCUMENT 12. EXPLANATORY REPORT ON DRAFT TREATY OF THE 'FOUCHET COMMITTEE' ON POLITICAL UNION, 15 MARCH 1962

Text Proposed by the French Delegation	*Text Proposed by the Delegations of Belgium, The Federal Republic of Germany, Italy, Luxembourg and the Netherlands*
Draft Treaty for the establishment of a union of States	Draft Treaty for the establishment of a union of States and of European peoples
PREAMBLE	PREAMBLE

(*Joint text*)

The High Contracting Parties,
   convinced that the union of Europe in freedom and respect for its diversity will permit its civilization to develop, add to the prestige of its spiritual heritage, increase its capacity to defend itself against external threats, facilitate the contribution it makes to the progress of other peoples and contribute [in

keeping with the principles of the United Nations Charter][1] to world peace;

affirming their attachment to the principles of democracy, to respect for law and to social justice;

resolved jointly to safeguard the dignity, freedom and equality of men, regardless of their status race or creed;

resolved to pursue the task of reconciling their essential interests already initiated, in their respective fields, by the European Coal and Steel Community, the European Economic Community and the European Atomic Energy Community;

resolved to pursue the task of reconciling their essential interests, already the objective, in their respective fields, of the European Coal and Steel Community, the European Economic Community and the European Atomic Energy Community, in order to lay the foundation for a destiny to be irrevocably shared;

(Joint text)

[desirous of welcoming] [ready to welcome] to their ranks other countries of Europe that are prepared to accept in every sphere the same responsibilities and the same obligations [and conscious of thus forming the nucleus of a union, membership of which will be open to other peoples of Europe that are as yet unable to take such a decision];

resolved, to this end, to give statutory form to the union of their peoples, in accordance with the declaration of 18 July 1961 by the Heads of State or Government;

Have appointed as their Plenipotentiaries:

. . . . . .

who, having exchanged their Full Powers, found in good and due form, have agreed as follows:

(Joint text)

TITLE I

Union of the European peoples

Article 1

By the present Treaty, a union of States [and of European peoples], hereafter called 'the European Union', is established.

[1] NOTE: The square brackets in this text enclose phrases regarding which the various delegations failed to agree.

The European Union is based on the principle of the equality of the rights and obligations of its members.

Article 2

It shall be the aim of the Union to reconcile, co-ordinate and unify the policy of Member States in spheres of common interest: foreign policy, economics, cultural affairs and defence.

Article 2

1. It shall be the task of the European Union to promote the unity of Europe by reconciling, co-ordinating and unifying the policy of Member States.

2. For the purpose of accomplishing this task, the objectives of the Union shall be:

— the adoption of a common foreign policy;
— the adoption of a common defence policy
  [within the framework of the Atlantic Alliance]
  [as a contribution towards strengthening the Atlantic Alliance];
— close co-operation in the educational, scientific and cultural fields;
— the harmonization and unification of the laws of Member States;
— the settlement, in a spirit of mutual understanding and constructive co-operation, of any differences that may arise in relations between Member States.

3. Objectives other than those laid down in the preceding paragraph may be defined by the Council after consultation with the European Parliament.

4. This Treaty shall not derogate from the competence of the European Communities.

(*Joint text*)

Article 3

There shall be solidarity and reciprocal assistance as between Member States. They undertake to co-operate to the full in pursuing the objectives of the European Union and in facilitating the accomplishment of its task.

(*Joint text*)

Article 4

The European Union shall have legal personality.

The Union shall enjoy in each of the Member States the most extensive legal capacity accorded to legal persons under their domestic law.

TITLE II
Institutions of the Union
Article 5

The Institutions of the Union shall be as follows:
— the Council;
— the Committees of Ministers;
— the Political Commission;
— the European Parliament.

TITLE II
Institutions of the Union
Article 5

1. The Institutions of the European Union shall be as follows:
— the Council and the Committees of Ministers;
— the European Parliament;
— the Court of Justice.

2. The Council and the Committees of Ministers shall be assisted by a Political Commission and a Secretary-General.

Article 6

The Council shall consist of the Heads of State or Government of Member States. It shall meet in principle every four months and not less than three times a year.

Article 6

1. The Council shall consist of the representatives of the Member States. Member States shall be represented on the Council, in accordance with the constitutional requirements and the usage prevailing in each country, by the Heads of State or Government and, where appropriate, by the Foreign Ministers.

2. The Council shall meet in ordinary session three times a year and in principle every four months. Extraordinary sessions of the Council may be convened at any time by its President on his own initiative or at the request of one or more Member States of the European Union.

3. The office of the President shall be exercised in rotation by each member of the Council for a term of [six months] [one year].

4. The Council shall lay down its own rules of procedure.

Article 7

The Council shall deliberate on questions whose inclusion on its agenda is requested by one or more Member States. The agenda shall be drawn up by the President. The Council shall adopt decisions necessary for achieving the aims of the Union unanimously. The Council's decisions shall be binding on Member States. The abstention of one or of two members shall not prevent a decision from being taken.

The decisions of the Council shall be implemented by Member States that have participated in their adoption. Member States that are not bound by a decision, by reason of their absence or abstention, may endorse it at any time. From the moment they endorse it, the decision shall be binding on them.

Article 7

1. The Council shall deliberate on all questions whose inclusion on the agenda is requested by one or more Member States or by the Secretary-General under the terms of Article 2. The agenda shall be drawn up by the President.

The meetings of the Council shall be prepared by the Committee of Foreign Ministers. Decisions necessary for achieving the aims of the European Union shall be passed by the Council unanimously.

2. The decisions of the Council shall be carried out in accordance with the constitutional requirements in force in each Member State. The Council may, by a unanimous decision, waive the principle of unanimity in specific cases. The abstention of one or of two members shall not prevent decisions requiring unanimity from being taken.

3. If a decision that requires unanimity cannot be adopted because it is opposed by one Member State, the Council shall adjourn the deliberation to a later date to be specified by it. Before this second deliberation takes place, the Council may decide to obtain the opinion of the European Parliament.

Article 8

1. The Council may conclude agreements on behalf of the European Union with Member States, third countries or international organizations. It shall lay down the

methods to be followed in its rules of procedure.

2. The agreements shall be submitted to the Parliament for an opinion. They shall not come into force until they have been approved in all Member States by the bodies that, under the respective constitutional requirements, must, where appropriate, approve such agreements concluded by these States.

3. Agreements concluded in accordance with the preceding provisions shall be binding on the institutions of the European Union and on Member States.

Article 8   *Article 9*

(Joint text)

1. The following committees shall be set up:
— a Committee of Foreign Ministers;
— a Committee of Ministers for Defence and for the Armed Forces;
— a Committee of Ministers of Education or of Ministers responsible for international cultural relations. The competence of this Committee shall be governed, without prejudice to the provisions of this Treaty, by the Convention embodying the Statute of the European Cultural Council and the annexed Conventions which as a whole are to be regarded as an integral part of this Treaty.

The Council may decide to set up other Committees of Ministers.

2. The Council may set up other Committees of Ministers.

3. The Committees enumerated above shall meet not less than four times a year and report to the Council.

Article 9

The Political Commission shall consist of representatives appointed by each Member State. It shall prepare the deliberations of the Council and ensure that its decisions

Article 10

The Political Commission shall consist of senior officials appointed by each State. This Commission shall prepare the deliberations of the Council and of the Committees are carried out. It shall perform such other duties as the Council decides to entrust to it. It shall have at its disposal the necessary staff and departments.

of Ministers and perform the duties which the Council decides to entrust to it.

Article 11

1. The Council shall appoint for a period of........ a Secretary-General who shall be independent of the Governments of the Member States of the European Union. His term of office shall be renewable.

2. He shall be assisted in the performance of his duties by a staff appointed by him in accordance with a procedure to be laid down, on his proposal, by the Council.

3. The functions of the Secretary-General and of members of the Secretariat shall be deemed to be incompatible with the exercise of any other office.

4. In the performance of their duties, the Secretary-General and the members of the Secretariat shall neither solicit nor accept instructions from any government. They shall abstain from any act that is incompatible with the nature of their functions.

5. The Member States undertake to respect the independence of the Secretary-General and of his staff and to refrain from influencing them in the accomplishment of their task.

Article 10

Article 12

(*Joint text*)

1. The parliamentary institution of the European Union shall be the Parliament provided for under Article 1 of the Convention relating to certain institutions common to the European Communities signed in Rome on 25 March 1957.

2. In fields that relate to the aims of the European Union,

the Parliament [or its members] may address questions to the Council.

3. In the same fields, the Parliament may submit recommendations to the Council.

4. The Council, on receipt of a question or of a recommendation from the European Parliament, shall make known at its next meeting what action it has taken in respect thereof.

Article 11   *Article 13*

(*Joint text*)

The Council shall each year submit to the European Parliament [a report] [a communication] on its activities.

The Council shall be represented at the debates held on [its report] [its communication].

The Council and the European Parliament shall jointly lay down the procedure for their collaboration.

Article 14

1. The Court of Justice of the European Communities shall be competent to decide on any dispute between Member States connected with the interpretation or application of this Treaty.

Member States undertake not to subject such disputes to any other form of settlement.

2. The Court of Justice of the European Communities shall be competent:

(a) to decide on any dispute between Member States where the said dispute is submitted to the Court under a special agreement between them;

(b) to give a decision pursuant to any arbitration clause contained in a contract, whether governed by public law or private law, concluded by or on behalf of the European Union.

TITLE IV
Finances of the European Union

TITLE IV
Finances of the European Union

Article 12   *Article 15*
(*Joint text*)

1. The budget of the European Union shall be drawn up annually. The financial year shall run from 1 January to 31 December inclusive.

2. The Council shall lay down the financial regulations of the European Union.

3. The draft budget, drawn up by the Political Commission, shall be adopted by the Council which may, where appropriate, make such amendments as it considers necessary.

3. The draft budget, drawn up by the Secretary-General with the assistance of the Political Commission, shall be adopted by the Council, after obtaining the Parliament's opinion.

Article 13   *Article 16*
(*Joint text*)

1. The administrative expenditure of the European Union shall be met from contributions by the Member States calculated according to the following scale:

[Belgium – – – – – 7·9
France – – – – – 28
Federal Republic of Germany – 28
Italy – – – – – 28
Luxembourg – – – – 0·2
Netherlands – – – – 7·9]

2. In the event of the accession of a further State, this scale shall be adjusted by decision of the Council.

3. A study shall be made, within the framework of the general review referred to in Article 20, of the conditions under which the contributions of Member States could be replaced or supplemented by the European Union's own resources.

Article 14   *Article 17*
The budget shall be implemented by the Political Commission.

The budget shall be implemented by the Secretary-General.

TITLE V
General provisions
Article 18
The European Union shall enjoy on the territory of Member States such privileges and immunities as

are necessary for it to accomplish its task under the conditions stipulated in a separate protocol which forms part of this Treaty. This shall also define the contractual and non-contractual liability of the European Union and the principles which shall govern its relations with its staff.

Article 15

This Treaty may be reviewed. Draft amendments shall be submitted to the Council by the Governments of the Member States.

Draft amendments adopted unanimously by the Council shall be submitted for ratification to the Member States, after the European Parliament, where appropriate, has expressed its opinion. They shall come into force once all the Member States have ratified them.

Article 19

1. This Treaty may be reviewed, without prejudice to the general review referred to in Article 20.

2. Draft amendments shall be submitted to the Council either by the Member States or by the Parliament. If the Council, after having consulted the Parliament where a draft is proposed by one of the Member States, unanimously adopts such a draft amendment, this shall be submitted to Member States for ratification.

Such draft amendment shall come into force when all the Member States have ratified it in accordance with their respective constitutional requirements.

Article 16

Three years after this Treaty comes into force, it shall be subjected to a review in order to consider suitable measures either for strengthening the Union in general in the light of progress already made or, in particular, for simplifying, rationalizing and co-ordinating the ways in which Member States co-operate.

Article 20

1. At the time fixed for the transition from the second to the third stage laid down in the Treaty establishing the European Economic Community, the present Treaty shall be subjected to a general review. This shall aim at determining suitable measures for strengthening the European Union and the powers of its institutions in the light of the progress already made.

With this end in view, a draft constitution of the European Union shall be drawn up by the Council before expiry of the time-limit specified above, and submitted to the European Parliament for its opinion.

2. The general review shall in particular have the following objectives:

(a) To associate the European Parliament more closely with the work of defining the common policy and carrying out the provisions of Article 138 of the Treaty establishing the European Economic Community relating to the election of the Parliament by direct universal suffrage;

(b) To gradually introduce the majority principle in decisions of the Council of the Union.

3. At the time of the general review, the conditions shall be fixed under which, at the end of the transition period of the Common Market, the European Union and the European Communities will be incorporated in an organic institutional framework, without prejudice to the machinery provided for in the Treaties of Paris and Rome. To facilitate this process, reforms shall be undertaken, in accordance with the procedures laid down in the Treaties of Paris and Rome and before the general review is carried out, with a view to simplifying and rationalizing the machinery provided for in those Treaties.

4. The competence of the Court of Justice shall be extended in the light of reforms introduced by the general review.

Article 17   *Article 21*

(*Joint text*)

The Union shall be open for membership to States that have

118

acceded to the European Communities referred to in the Preamble to this Treaty.

The admission of a new State shall be decided unanimously by the Council after an additional Act to this Treaty has been drawn up.	Accession shall come into effect once the State concerned has submitted the instrument ratifying this Act.

Article 18   *Article 22*

(Joint text)

The rules governing the language of the European Union shall without prejudice to the rules of procedure of the European Parliament and of the Court, be determined by unanimous decision of the Council.

Article 19   *Article 23*

(Joint text)

This Treaty shall be ratified. The instruments of ratification shall be deposited with . . . . . which shall notify the Governments of the other Member States that this has been done.

This Treaty shall come into force on the day when the instrument of ratification is deposited by the last signatory State to do so.

Article 20   *Article 24*

(Joint text)

1. This Treaty is drawn up in a single original in Dutch, French, German and Italian, which shall be the official working languages of the Institutions of the European Union. All four texts, which are equally authentic, shall be deposited in the archives of the Government of . . . . . which shall transmit a certified copy to each of the Governments of the other signatory States.

DOCUMENT 13. EXTRACTS FROM THE TREATY ESTABLISHING A SINGLE COUNCIL AND A SINGLE COMMISSION OF THE EUROPEAN COMMUNITIES SIGNED IN BRUSSELS, 8 APRIL 1965

Chapter 1. The Council of the European Communities

Article 1. A Council of the European Communities, hereinafter referred to as 'the Council', is hereby established. This Council shall take the place of the Special Council of Ministers of the European Coal and Steel Community, of the Council of the European Economic Community and of the Council of the European Atomic Energy Community.

The Council shall exercise the powers and competences developing upon these institutions under the conditions laid down in the Treaties establishing respectively the European Coal and Steel Community, the European Economic Community and the European Atomic Energy Community, as also in the present Treaty.

Article 2. The Council shall consist of representatives of the Member States. Each Government shall delegate to it one of its members.

The Office of the President shall be exercised for a term of six months by each member of the Council in rotation and in the following order: Belgium, Germany, France, Italy, Luxembourg, the Netherlands.

Article 3. Meetings of the Council shall be called by the President on his own initiative, or at the request of a member or of the Commission.

Article 4. A Committee consisting of the Permanent Representatives of the Member States shall prepare the work of the Council and carry out the latter's mandates. . . .

Chapter II. The Commission of the European Communities

Article 9. A Commission of the European Communities, hereinafter referred to as 'the Commission', is hereby established. This Commission shall take the place of the High Authority of the European Coal and Steel Community, of the Commission of the European Economic Community and of the Commission of the European Atomic Energy Community.

The Commission shall exercise the powers and competences devolving upon these institutions under the conditions laid down in the Treaties establishing respectively the European Coal and Steel Community, the European Economic Community and the European Atomic Energy Community, as also in the present Treaty.

Article 10. (1) The Commission shall consist of nine members, who shall be chosen on the grounds of their general competence, and whose independence can be fully guaranteed.

The number of members of the Commission may be amended by the Council, acting unanimously.

Only nationals of Member States may be members of the Commission.

The Commission must include at least one national of each of the Member States, but the number of members who are nationals of one and the same State shall not exceed two.

(2) The members of the Commission shall act completely independently in the performance of their duties, in the general interest of the Communities.

In the performance of their duties, they shall neither seek nor take instructions from any Government or other body. They shall refrain from any action incompatible with the nature of their duties. Each Member State undertakes to respect this principle and not to seek to influence the Members of the Commission in the performance of their duties.

The members of the Commission may not, during their term of office, engage in any other paid or unpaid occupation. When entering upon their duties, they shall give a solemn undertaking that both during and after their term of office, they will respect the obligations arising therefrom, and in particular their duty to exercise honesty and discretion as regards the acceptance, after their term of office, of certain appointments or benefits. In the event of any breach of these obligations, the Court of Justice, on the application of the Council or of the Commission, may, according to the circumstances, order that the member concerned either be compulsorily retired in accordance with the provisions of Article 13 or forfeit his right to a pension or other benefits in lieu thereof.

Article 11. The members of the Commission shall be appointed by mutual agreement between the Governments of the Member States.

Their term of office shall be for a period of four years. It shall be renewable.

Article 12. Apart from death and retirement in rotation, termination of appointment of a member of the Commission shall occur by voluntary resignation or compulsory retirement.

A vacancy thus caused shall be filled for the remainder of the retiring member's term of office. The Council may unanimously decide that such a vacancy need not be filled.

Unless he is compulsorily retired in accordance with the provisions of Article 13, a member of the Commission shall remain in office until his successor's appointment.

Article 13. If any member of the Commission no longer fulfils the conditions required for the performance of his duties or if he has been guilty of serious misconduct, the Court of Justice, on the application of the Council or of the Commission, may compulsorily retire him from office.

Article 14. The President and the three Vice-Presidents of the Commission shall be appointed from among its members for a term of two years in accordance with the same procedure as that laid down for the appointment of the members of the Commission. Their term of office shall be renewable.

Save where the whole Commission is replaced, the Commission shall be consulted before such appointments are made.

In the event of resignation or death, the President and the Vice-Presidents shall be replaced for the remainder of their terms of office in accordance with the above provisions.

Article 15. The Council and the Commission shall consult together and shall decide on methods of collaboration by mutual agreement.

Article 16. The Commission shall adopt rules of procedure to ensure that both it and its administrative services operate in accordance with the terms of the Treaties establishing the European Coal and Steel Community, the European Economic Community and the European Atomic Energy Community as also of the present Treaty. It shall ensure that its rules of procedure are published.

Article 17. The Commission shall reach its conclusions by a majority of the number of members provided for in Article 10.

A meeting of the Commission shall only be valid if the number of members laid down in its rules of procedure is present.

Article 18. The Commission shall publish annually, not later than one month before the opening of the session of the Assembly, a general report on the activities of the Communities . . .

Article 32. (1) Until the date of entry into force of the Treaty establishing a single European Community and for a period not exceeding three years from the appointment of its members, the Commission shall consist of fourteen members.

During this period, the number of members who are nationals of one and the same State shall not exceed three.

(2) The President, the Vice-Presidents and the members of the Commission shall be appointed on the entry into force of this Treaty. The Commission shall take up its duties on the fifth day following the appointment of its members. The term of office of the members of the High Authority and of the Commissions of the European Economic Community and of the European Atomic Energy Community shall at the same time be terminated . . .

DOCUMENT 14. EXTRACT FROM THE STATEMENT BY PRESIDENT DE GAULLE AT HIS PRESS CONFERENCE HELD IN PARIS ON 9 SEPTEMBER 1965

What happened in Brussels on June 30, in connection with the agricultural financing regulation, highlighted not only the persistent reluctance of the majority of our partners to bring agriculture within the scope of the Common Market, but also certain mistakes or ambiguities in the Treaties setting up the economic union of the Six. That is why the crisis was, sooner or later, inevitable.

The three Treaties, forming the ECSC, Euratom and the Common Market respectively, were concluded before the French recovery of 1958. They also take account above all of what the other countries wanted. Thus, the ECSC, independently of the Franco-German *rapprochement* which it was intended to bring about, involved, essentially, returning control of its coal and steel to Germany and giving Italy, which has no natural coal and steel resources, the chance to build itself, in its turn, a major metallurgical industry. As for Euratom, that institution was intended to pool all that had been done in the field of nuclear energy—of which France, because of the lead she had gained, was to make the largest contribution—and then to control the output of fissionable materials in order to hinder its military use, when ours was the only country among the Six undertaking the manufacture of nuclear weapons. Lastly, the Rome Treaty regulated very fully the industrial community in which our neighbours were particularly interested, but not at all the agricultural common market in which we were the most concerned.

Moreover, they each set up an executive structure in the form of a commission independent of the member states, even though the members were appointed and paid by them, and a legislative structure under the auspices of an assembly composed of members from the various national parliaments, even though their electors had given them no mandate except in the national sphere. This embryonic technocracy, for the most part foreign, was certain to encroach upon French democracy, in dealing with problems which determine the very existence of our country, and it obviously could not be allowed to conduct our affairs once we had decided to take our destiny into our own hands.

Who can possibly not be aware that we have championed for a long time the idea of grouping together, for economic and, I add, political purposes, the states of Western Europe? To recognize this, one only has to look up the statements made on this subject on many important occasions during and immediately after the last war, at a time when no one else was talking about it, and also all the practical steps taken towards this end taken by my Government. As far as the economy is concerned, we believe it is true that the systematic organization of the respective activities of the countries lying round the Rhine and the Alps corresponds to the facts that they are close neighbours, that their production is at the same time analogous and complementary, and that it is in keeping with the needs of our times to form units on a broader basis than that of the individual European states. Furthermore, France, which is booming and whose currency has become one of the strongest in the world, has every reason to renounce its old protectionism and gradually to open itself up to competition. That is why, for the past seven years, we have very actively helped to build up the European Community, formed in theory in 1957, but existing only on paper until 1959 because the chronic deficit in the French balance of payments stopped the organization from getting off the ground, except in speeches.

What we wanted yesterday, and what we want today, is a Community which is both equitable and reasonable.

Equitable: that means that, taking account of their particular circumstances, agricultural products should be subject to the Common Market at the same time as industrial products. Reasonable: that means that nothing of any importance, either in the initial planning or the later operation of the Common Market, should be decided, and certainly not applied, except by the responsible authorities in the six countries, that is to say, the national governments subject to parliamentary control. But we know—and heaven knows how well we know it—that there is a different conception of a European federation in which, according to the dreams of those who have conceived it, the member countries would lose their national identities, and which, moreover, in the absence of a federator such as Caesar and his successors, Charlemagne, the Emperors Otto and Charles V, Napoleon and Hitler each tried to become in the West— n his own fashion—and such as Stalin tried to become in the East, would be ruled by some sort of technocratic body of elders, stateless and irresponsible.

One knows also that, in opposition to this project devoid of all realism, France proposed a plan for organized co-operation between the states, evolving no doubt towards a confederation. This plan alone appears to her to correspond to what the nations of our Continent really are. This plan alone would one day permit other countries like England and Spain to join in, because these countries, like ourselves, do not wish to lose their sovereignty. It alone would make an *entente* of the whole of Europe conceivable one day.

However, and whatever the reservations about the political theories involved, it looked as if the very long and detailed negotiations at Brussels were on the point of being concluded. Certainly, we had had the greatest difficulty in getting our partners—in practice—to admit that farm produce should form an integral part of the Community. Well, as everyone is aware, this is for us a *sine qua non* condition, for, if it were not fulfilled, we should remain burdened with the very heavy cost—much greater than that of our neighbours—of supporting our agriculture, and we should consequently be handicapped in industrial competition, too. That is why we were only able to agree, in January 1962, that the Community pass into the second phase of the Treaty, which involved reduction in customs duties, on the condition of a formal commitment to settle the agricultural problem, particularly from the financial point of view, by June 30 of this year at the latest, and under conditions and following a timetable precisely laid down. Although at the time there were some tears and grinding of teeth, we were able at the last moment to gain the agreement of our partners, and we had the right to believe that they would meet their commitments by the agreed deadline.

Whilst observing that the cumbersome international machinery built at great cost around the Commission frequently duplicated the qualified services of the six governments, we noted the competence of these officials on the basis of their work and observed that they refrained from excessive encroachments upon the only valid powers, which are the individual states.

It was too good to last! In Brussels, on June 30, our delegation came up against a serious stumbling-block concerning the final definition of the financial regulation, as previously agreed on. Shortly before, the Commission had suddenly abandoned its political discretion and formulated terms in connection with this financial regulation whereby it would have a budget of its own, possibly of up to 20,000 million new francs ($4,000 million), the states having made over into its hands the levies and customs receipts which would literally have made it a great independent financial power. And then those very states, having fed these enormous amounts to it at the expense of their tax-payers, would have no way of supervising it.

It is true that the authors of the plan alleged that the budget would be submitted to the Assembly for consideration. But intervention by this Assembly, which is essentially an advisory body, the members of which were in no way elected for this purpose, would merely aggravate the nature of the usurpation of powers which was being demanded. Finally, regardless of whether or not there was premeditated collusion with the Commission's supranational claims, the attitude adopted by certain delegations (who stated their readiness to approve and support these claims), and finally the fact that some of our partners at the last moment went back on their undertakings, we had no alternative, in the circumstances, but to break off the Brussels negotiations.

I must add that in the light of this event we have been more clearly able to assess in what position our country risks finding itself if some of the provisions initially laid down in the Rome Treaty were actually enforced. It is on the basis of this text that from January 1 next the decisions in the Council of Ministers would be decided by majority vote; in other words, France would be exposed to the possibility of being overruled in any economic matter, whatsoever, and therefore in social and sometimes political matters, and that, in particular, all that has been achieved by French agriculture could be threatened at any moment, without France's let or leave. Moreover, after this same date, the proposals made by the Commission in Brussels would have to be accepted or rejected in their entirety by the Council of Ministers, without the states being able to change anything, unless by some extraordinary chance, the six states were unanimous in formulating an amendment. We know that the members of the Commission, although appointed by agreement among the governments, are no longer responsible to them, and that, even on the conclusion of their terms of office, they can only be replaced by the unanimous agreement of the Six, which, in effect, renders them immovable. One can see where such a subordinate position could lead us, if we allowed ourselves to deny, at one and the same time, our freedom of action and our Constitution, which lays down that 'French sovereignty resides in the French people, which exercises it through its representatives and by means of referenda', without making any sort of exception at all.

That is the position. There is no doubt that it is conceivable and desirable that the great undertaking that is the Community should one day be got under way again. But that can take place, probably, only after a period of time the length of which no one can foresee. Who knows, in fact, if, when and how the policies of each one of our partners, after some electoral or parliamentary development, will not finally come round to facing the facts which have once more come to the fore.

However that may be, France for her part is ready to join in all exchanges of views on this subject which are proposed by the other governments. Should the occasion arise, she envisages the reopening of negotiations at Brussels as soon as agriculture is brought fully within the scope of the Common Market, and as soon as people are ready to have done with the pretensions which ill-founded, utopian myths raise up against common sense and reality.

DOCUMENT 15. EXTRACTS FROM THE STATEMENT ISSUED AFTER THE MINISTERIAL MEETING BETWEEN THE SIX GOVERNMENTS HELD IN LUXEMBOURG ON 28–29 JANUARY 1966

MAJORITY VOTING

1. When issues very important to one or more member countries are at stake, the members of the Council will try, within a reasonable time, to reach solutions which can be adopted by all the members of the Council, while respecting their mutual interests, and those of the Community, in accordance with Article 2 of the Treaty.

2. The French delegation considers that, when very important issues are at stake, the discussion must be continued until unanimous agreement is reached.

3. The six delegations note that there is a divergence of views on what should be done in the event of a failure to reach complete agreement.

4. However, they consider that this divergence does not prevent the Community's work being resumed in accordance with the normal procedure . . .

PART III

The Community and Africa

MARIANNE: 'But of course my little ones do form part of the family....'

DOCUMENT 16

PREAMBLE

His Majesty the King of the Belgians,
The President of the Federal Republic of Germany,
The President of the French Republic,
The President of the Republic of Italy,
Her Royal Highness the Grand Duchess of Luxembourg,
Her Majesty the Queen of the Netherlands,

Contracting Parties to the Treaty establishing the European Economic Community signed at Rome on 25 March 1957 and hereinafter designated 'the Treaty', whose States are hereinafter referred to as 'Member States'

and the Council of the European Economic Community of the first part, and

His Majesty the Mwami of Burundi,
The President of the Federal Republic of Cameroon,
The President of the Central African Republic,
The President of the Republic of Chad,
The President of the Republic of the Congo (Brazzaville),
The President of the Republic of the Congo (Léopoldville),
The President of the Republic of Dahomey,
The President of the Gabon Republic,
The President of the Republic of the Ivory Coast,
The President of the Republic of Madagascar,
The Head of State, President of the Council of the Government of the Republic of Mali,
The President of the Islamic Republic of Mauritania,
The President of the Republic of Niger,
The President of the Republic of Rwanda,
The President of the Republic of Senegal,
The President of the Republic of Somalia,
The President of the Republic of Togo,
The President of the Republic of the Upper Volta,

whose States are hereinafter referred to as 'Associated States' of the second part,

Having regard to the Treaty establishing the European Economic Community,

Reaffirming accordingly their desire to maintain their Association,

Wishing to demonstrate their common desire for co-operation on the basis of complete equality and friendly relations, observing the principles of the United Nations Charter,

Resolved to develop economic relations between the Associated States and the Community,

Determined to pursue their efforts together with a view to the economic, social and cultural progress of their countries,

Desirous of furthering the industrialization of the Associated States and the diversification of their economies, with a view to enabling them to strengthen their economic independence and stability,

Conscious of the importance of developing inter-African trade and co-operation as well as international economic relations,

Have decided to conclude a new Convention of Association between the Community and the Associated States . . .

TITLE I. TRADE

Article 1. With a view to promoting an increase of trade between the Associated States and the Member States, strengthening their economic relations and the economic independence of the Associated States and thereby contributing to the development of international trade, the High Contracting Parties have agreed upon the following provisions which shall regulate their mutual trade relations.

Chapter 1. Customs duties and quantitative restrictions

Article 2. (1) Goods originating in Associated States shall, when imported into Member States, benefit from the progressive abolition of customs duties and charges having an effect equivalent to such duties, resulting between Member States under the provisions of Articles 12, 13, 14, 15 and 17 of the Treaty and the decisions which have been or may be adopted to accelerate the rate of achieving the aims of the Treaty.

(2) Nevertheless, upon the entry into force of the Convention, Member States shall abolish the customs duties and charges having an effect equivalent to such duties which they apply to the goods originating in Associated States which are listed in the Annex to this Convention.

At the same time Member States shall apply the common customs tariff duties of the Community to imports of these goods from third countries.

(3) Imports from third countries of unroasted coffee into the Benelux countries on the one hand, and of bananas into the Federal Republic of Germany on the other hand, shall be subject to the terms set out respectively, as to unroasted coffee, in the Protocol this day concluded between the Member States and, as to bananas, in the Protocol concluded on 25 March 1957 between the Member States and in the Declaration annexed to this Convention.

(4) Application of the provisions of this Article shall not pre-determine the treatment to be applied to certain agricultural products under the provisions of Article 11 of this Convention.

(5) At the request of an Associated State, there shall be consultations within the Association Council regarding the conditions of application of this Article.

Article 3. (1) Each Associated State shall accord identical tariff treatment of goods originating in any of the Member States; Associated States not applying this rule on the entry into force of this Convention shall do so within the following six months.

(2) In each Associated State goods originating in Member States shall benefit, under the terms set out in Protocol No. 1 annexed to this Convention, from the progressive abolition of customs duties and charges having an effect equivalent to such duties which that Associated State applies to imports of these goods into its territory.

Provided always that each Associated State may retain or introduce customs duties and charges having an effect equiv-alent to such duties which correspond to its development needs or its industrialization requirements or which are intended to contribute to its budget.

The customs duties and charges having an effect equivalent

to such duties levied by Associated States in accordance with the foregoing sub-paragraph, as also any alteration which they may make in these duties and charges under the provisions of Protocol No. 1, may not either *de jure* or *de facto* give rise to any direct or indirect discrimination between Member States.

3. At the request of the Community and in accordance with the procedures laid down in Protocol No. 1, there shall be consultations within the Association Council regarding the conditions of application of this Article.

Article 4. (1) Insofar as an Associated State levies export duties on exports of its products to Member States, these duties may not give rise, *de jure* or *de facto*, to any direct or indirect discrimination between Member States and may not be greater than those applied to products exported to the most favoured third country.

(2) Without prejudice to the application of Article 13, paragraph 2 of this Convention, the Association Council shall take suitable measures if the application of such duties leads to serious disturbances in the conditions of competition.

Article 5. (1) With regard to the abolition of quantitative restrictions, Member States shall apply to imports of goods originating in the Associated States the relevant provisions of the Treaty, and of the decisions which have been or may be adopted to accelerate the rate of achieving the aims of the Treaty, which they apply in their relations with each other.

(2) At the request of an Associated State, there shall be consultations within the Association Council regarding the conditions of application of this Article.

Article 6. (1) Associated States shall, not later than four years after the entry into force of the Convention, abolish all quantitative restrictions on imports of goods originating in Member States and all measures having equivalent effect. This abolition shall be carried out progressively under the conditions set out in Protocol No. 2 annexed to this Convention.

2. Associated States shall refrain from introducing any new quantitative restrictions or measures having equivalent effect on imports of goods originating in Member States.

(3) Should the measures provided for in Article 3 prove insufficient to meet their development needs and their in-

dustrialization requirements, or in the event of difficulties in their balance of payments, or, where agricultural products are concerned, in connection with the requirements arising from existing regional market organizations, Associated States may, notwithstanding the provisions of the two foregoing paragraphs and subject to the terms of Protocol No. 2, retain or introduce quantitative restrictions on imports of goods originating in Member States.

(4) Associated States in which imports come within the province of a State trading monopoly or of any body which, *de jure* or *de facto*, either directly or indirectly limits, controls, directs or influences them, shall take any steps necessary to attain the objectives defined in this Title and to abolish progressively any discrimination in conditions of supply and marketing of goods.

Without prejudice to the application of Article 7 below, foreign trade plans drawn up by the Associated States shall not contain or bring about, *de jure* or *de facto*, any direct or indirect discrimination between Member States.

The Associated States concerned shall inform the Association Council of the steps taken to implement the provisions of this paragraph.

(5) At the request of the Community, there shall be consultations within the Association Council regarding the conditions of application of this Article.

Article 7. Without prejudice to the special provisions for border trade, the treatment that the Associated States apply by virtue of this Title to goods originating in Member States shall in no case be less favourable than that applied to goods originating in the most favoured third country.

Article 8. This Convention shall not preclude the maintenance or establishment of customs unions or free-trade areas among Associated States.

Article 9. This Convention shall not preclude the maintenance or establishment of customs union or free-trade areas between one or more Associated States and one or more third countries insofar as they neither are nor prove to be incompatible with the principles and provisions of the said Convention.

Article 10. The provisions of the foregoing Articles 3, 4 and 9 shall not preclude prohibitions or restrictions on imports, exports or goods in transit justified on grounds of public morality, public policy, public security, the protection of human, animal or plant life or health, the protection of national treasures possessing artistic, historic or archaeological value, or the protection of industrial and commercial property. Provided always that such prohibitions or restrictions shall not be used as a means of arbitrary discrimination nor as a disguised restriction on trade.

Chapter II. *Provisions concerning certain agricultural products*

Article 11. When drawing up its common agricultural policy, the Community shall take the interests of the Associated States into consideration as regards products similar to and competitive with European products. The Community and the Associated States concerned shall consult together for this purpose.

The treatment applicable to imports into the Community of these products, if they have originated in the Associated States, shall be determined by the Community in the course of defining its common agricultural policy, after consultation within the Association Council.

Chapter III. *Provisions concerning commercial policy*

Article 12. (1) On matters of commercial policy, the Contracting Parties agree to keep each other informed and, should one of them so request, to consult together for the purpose of giving good effect to this Convention.

(2) Such consultation shall bear on measures concerning trade with third countries if these measures are likely to harm the interests of one or more Contracting Parties, with particular reference to :

(a) the suspension, alteration or abolition of customs duties,

(b) the granting of tariff quotas at reduced or zero duties, other than the quotas referred to in Article 2, paragraph 3, above,

(c) the introduction, reduction or abolition of quantitative restrictions, without prejudice to the obligations incumbent upon certain Contracting Parties by reason of their membership of GATT.

(3) Upon the entry into force of this Convention, the Association Council shall define the procedure for consultation and exchange of information in respect of the implementation of this Article.

Chapter IV. *Safeguard Clauses*

Article 13. (1) If serious disturbances occur in one sector of the economy of an Associated State or jeopardize its external financial stability, that State may take the necessary protective measures, notwithstanding the provisions of Article 3, paragraph 2, sub-paragraph 1 and Article 6, paragraphs 1, 2 and 4.

The measures and the methods of applying them shall be notified immediately to the Association Council.

(2) If serious disturbance occur in one sector of the economy of the Community or of one or more Member States, or jeopardize their external financial stability, and if difficulties arise which may result in a region suffering grave economic hardship, the Community may take, or may authorize the Member State or States concerned to take such measures as may prove necessary in their relations with the Associated States, notwithstanding the provisions of Articles 2 and 5.

These measures and the methods of applying them shall be notified immediately to the Association Council.

(3) For the purpose of implementing paragraphs 1 and 2 of this Article, priority shall be given to such measures as will least disturb the functioning of the Association. These measures shall not exceed the limits strictly necessary to remedy the difficulties that have arisen.

(4) There shall be consultations within the Association Council regarding the measures taken under paragraphs 1 and 2 of this Article.

Such consultations shall be held at the request of the Community in respect of measures under paragraph 1 and at the request of one or more Associated States in respect of those under paragraph 2.

Chapter V. *General Provisions*

Article 14. Without prejudice to the special provisions laid down in this Convention, and particularly those of Article 3 above, each Contracting Party shall refrain from any measure or practice of an internal fiscal nature that directly or indirectly sets up any discrimination between its own products and similar products originating in the territories of the other Contracting Parties.

TITLE II. FINANCIAL AND TECHNICAL CO-OPERATION

Article 15. Under the conditions determined below the Community shall participate in measures calculated to promote the economic and social development of the Associated States, by supplementing the efforts achieved by those States.

Article 16. For the purposes set out in Article 15, and for the duration of this Convention, an aggregate amount of 730 million units of account shall be provided as follows:

(*a*) 666 million units of account by the Member States; this amount, to be paid into the European Development Fund, hereinafter referred to as 'the Fund', shall be employed up to 620 million units of account in the form of grants and the balance in the form of loans on special terms;

(*b*) up to 64 million units of account by the European Investment Bank, hereinafter referred to as 'the Bank', in the form of loans granted by it under the terms set out in Protocol No. 5 concerning the administration of the financial aids, annexed to this Convention.

Article 17. Under the terms laid down by this Convention and by Protocol No. 5, the amount fixed in Article 16 above shall be employed as follows:

1. in the field of economic and social investments,
   — for basic economic and social schemes,
   — for production schemes of general interest,
   — for production schemes providing normal financial returns,
   — for relevant technical assistance before, during and after such investments;
2. in the field of general technical co-operation,
   — for surveying the development prospects of the economies of the Associated States,

— for staff training and vocational training programmes;
3. in the field of aids for diversification and production,
   — for measures essentially intended to make marketing possible at competitive prices on the Community's markets as a whole, by encouraging, in particular, rationalization of cropping and sales methods, and by aiding producers to make the necessary adaptations;
4. in the field of price stabilization,
   — for advances for the purpose of helping to alleviate the effects of temporary fluctuations in world prices.

Article 18. Grants and loans shall be assigned as follows:

(*a*) up to 500 million units of account for financing the measures referred to in Article 17, paragraphs 1 and 2,

(*b*) up to 230 million units of account for financing the measures referred to in Article 17, paragraph 3.

Article 19. The Bank loans referred to in Article 16 (*b*) may carry a rebate on the interest. The rate of such rebates may be up to 3 per cent on loans of a maximum duration of 25 years.

The amounts required to pay such rebates shall, so long as the Fund exists, be charged to the amount of the grants provided for in Article 16 (*a*).

Article 20. (1) The Community may grant advances from the liquid assets of the Fund up to a ceiling of 50 million units of account for the operations provided for in Article 17, paragraph 4.

(2) Such advances shall be granted according to the terms set out in Protocol No. 5.

Article 21. In order to finance the measures referred to in Article 17, the Associated State or group of Associated States concerned shall, as prescribed in Protocol No. 5, open a file for each scheme or programme for which it is requesting financial assistance. It shall send this file to the Community, addressed to the Commission.

Article 22. The Community shall examine the requests for financing that are brought before it by virtue of the provisions of the foregoing Article. It shall maintain such contacts with the Associated States concerned as it may require in order that its decisions on the schemes or programmes submitted to it may be formulated in full knowledge of the facts. The Associated State or group of Associated States concerned shall be informed of the decision taken regarding its request.

Article 23. Aid contributed by the Community for the purpose of carrying out certain schemes or programmes may take the form of participation in financing in which, in particular, third countries, international finance organizations, or credit and development institutions and authorities, whether of the Associated States or the Member States, may take part.

Article 24. (1) The following shall be entitled to benefit from aids from the Fund:

(*a*) as regards grants:
— for economic and social investment schemes: either the Associated States, or legal persons who are non-profit-making in their main capacity, who have a status of general or social interest, and who are subject in those States to government inspection;
— for staff training and vocational training programmes and for economic surveys: the Governments of the Associated States specialized bodies and institutions; or, on exceptional grounds, scholars and trainees;
— for aid towards production: producers;
— for aid towards diversification: the Associated States, producer groups or similar bodies approved by the Community; or, failing these, producers themselves;
(*b*) as regards loans on special terms and rebates on interest:
— for economic and social investment schemes: either the Associated States, or legal persons who are non-profit-making in their main capacity, who have a status of general or social interest, and who are subject in those States to government inspection, or, possibly, private enterprises by special decision of the Community;
— for aid towards diversification: the Associated States, producer groups or similar bodies approved by the Community, or, failing these, producers themselves and, possibly, private enterprises by special decision of the Community.

(2) Financial aids may not be used to cover current administrative, maintenance and operating expenses.

Article 25. As regards operations financed by the Fund or by the Bank, participation in the letting out of contracts, invitations for tenders, purchasing and other contracts shall be open on equal terms, to all natural and legal persons who are nationals of the Member States or the Associated States.

Article 26. The amounts allocated for financing schemes or programmes, under the provisions of this Title, shall be utilized in accordance with the purposes decided upon and shall be expended to the best economic advantage.

Article 27. The Association Council shall lay down the general pattern for financial and technical co-operation within the framework of association, more particularly in the light of an annual report to be submitted to it by the organ responsible for administering the Community's financial and technical aid.

Article 28. If any Associated State should fail to ratify the Convention, under the terms set out in Article 57, or denounce the Convention in accordance with Article 60, it shall then be obligatory upon the Contracting Parties to adjust the amount of financial aid fixed in Articles 16 and 18.

TITLE III. RIGHT OF ESTABLISHMENT, SERVICES, PAYMENTS AND CAPITAL

Article 29. Without prejudice to measures adopted in implementation of the Treaty, in each Associated State nationals and companies of every Member State shall be placed on an equal footing as regards the right of establishment and provision of services, progressively and not later than three years after the entry into force of this Convention.

The Association Council may authorize an Associated State, at its request, to suspend implementation of the provisions of the foregoing sub-paragraph over a given period and for a given activity.

Nevertheless, in an Associated State nationals and companies of a Member State may benefit from the provisions of the first sub-paragraph, in respect of a given activity, only in so far as the State to which they belong grants similar advantages for the same activity to the nationals and companies of the Associated State in question.

Article 30. Should an Associated State grant nationals or companies of a State which is neither a Member State of the Community nor an Associated State within the meaning of this Convention, more favourable treatment than that which implementation of the provisions of this Title afford to nationals, such treatment shall be extended to nationals or companies of the Member States, excepting where it arises out of regional agreements.

Article 31. Subject to the provisions relating to movements of capital, the right of establishment within the meaning of this Convention shall include the right to engage in and carry on non-wage-earning activities, to set up and manage undertakings and in particular companies, and to set up agencies, branches or subsidiaries.

Article 32. Services within the meaning of this Convention shall be deemed to be services normally provided against remuneration, in so far as they are not governed by the provisions relating to trade, the right of establishment and movements of capital. Services shall include in particular activities of an industrial character, activities of a commercial character, artisan activities and activities of the liberal professions, excluding wage-earning activities.

Article 33. Companies within the meaning of this Convention shall be deemed to be companies under civil or commercial law, including co-operative societies and other legal persons under public or private law, but not including non-profit-making companies.

Companies of a Member State or an Associated State shall be companies constituted in accordance with the law of a Member State or an Associated State, and having their registered office, central administration, or main establishment in a Member State or an Associated State; nevertheless, should they have only their registered office in a Member State or an Associated State, their business must be actively and continuously linked with the economy of that Member State or Associated State.

Article 34. The Association Council shall take any decisions required to further the implementation of Articles 29 to 33 above.

Article 35. Each Signatory State undertakes, to the full extent of its powers, to authorize payments relating to trade in goods, services and capital and to wages, as also the transfer of such payments to the Member State or Associated State in which the creditor or the beneficiary is resident, in so far as the movement of such goods, services, capital or persons has been liberalized in implementation of this Convention.

Article 36. Throughout the whole duration of the loans and advances referred to in Chapters III, IV and V of Protocol No. 5, the Associated States undertake to make available to debtors the foreign currency necessary for the repayment of capital and interest on loans granted for schemes to be carried out in their territory and for repayment of advances granted to the stabilization funds.

Article 37. (1) Associated States shall make every endeavour not to introduce any new exchange restriction that would affect the treatment applied to investments and to current payments connected with the movements of capital resulting therefrom, where these are effected by persons residing in the Member States, and not to make the existing controls more restrictive.

(2) To the extent necessary for achieving the objectives of this Convention, the Associated States undertake to treat nationals and companies of Member States on an equal footing, not later than 1 January 1965, in respect of investments made by them as from the date of the entry into force of the Convention, as also of movements of capital resulting therefrom.

Article 38. The Association Council shall formulate any appropriate recommendations to the Contracting Parties concerning the implementation of Articles 35, 36 and 37 above.

TITLE IV. INSTITUTIONS OF THE ASSOCIATION

Article 39. The Institutions of the Association shall be:
— the Association Council assisted by the Association Committee,
— the Parliamentary Conference of the Association,
— the Court of Arbitration of the Association.

Article 40. The Association Council shall be composed, on the one hand, of the members of the Council of the European

Economic Community and members of the Commission of the European Economic Community and, on the other hand, of one member of the Government of each Associated State.

Any member of the Association Council prevented from attending may be represented. The representative shall exercise all the rights of the accredited member.

Proceedings of the Association Council shall only be valid if half the members of the Council of the Community, one member of the Commission and half the accredited members representing the Governments of the Associated States are present.

Article 41. The office of the President of the Association Council shall be exercised alternately by a member of the Council of the European Economic Community and a member of the Government of an Associated State.

Article 42. Meetings of the Association Council shall be called once a year by the President.

Furthermore it shall meet whenever necessary, in accordance with the conditions laid down in its rules of procedure.

Article 43. The Association Council shall express itself by mutual agreement between the Community on the one hand and the Associated States on the other.

The Community on the one hand and the Associated States on the other shall each by means of an internal Protocol determine their procedure for arriving at their respective positions.

Article 44. In cases covered by this Convention, the Association Council shall dispose of the power of decision; such decisions shall be binding upon the Contracting Parties, who shall be under the obligation to take all necessary measures to carry them out.

The Association Council may likewise formulate such resolutions, recommendations or opinions as it may deem necessary to achieve the common objectives and to ensure that the Association system works efficiently.

The Association Council shall periodically study the results of the Association system in the light of that system's objectives.

The Association Council shall lay down its rules of procedure.

Article 45. The Association Council shall be assisted in the performance of its task by an Association Committee composed on the one hand of one representative of each Member State and one representative of the Commission and, on the other, of one representative of each Associated State.

Article 46. The Office of the Chairman of the Association Committee shall be filled by the State which is presiding over the Association Council.

The Association Committee shall lay down its rules of procedure, which shall be submitted to the Association Council for approval.

Article 47. (1) In its rules of procedure the Association Council shall define the duties and powers of the Association Committee, with the object, in particular, of ensuring the continuity of co-operation essential to the satisfactory operation of the Association.

(2) The Association Council may when necessary delegate to the Association Committee the exercise of the powers entrusted to it by this Convention, under the terms and within the limits laid down by the Council.

In that event, the Committee shall give its decisions in accordance with the terms of Article 43.

Article 48. The Association Committee shall account for its actions to the Association Council, particularly in matters which have been the subject of a delegation of powers.

It shall also submit any useful proposal to the Association Council.

Article 49. The duties of the Secretariat of the Association Council and the Association Committee shall be carried out on a basis of parity and in accordance with the rules of procedure of the Association Council.

Article 50. The Parliamentary Conference of the Association shall meet once a year. It shall be composed, on a basis of parity, of members of the Assembly and members of the Parliaments of the Associated States.

Each year the Association Council shall submit a report on its activities to the Parliamentary Conference.

The Parliamentary Conference may vote resolutions on matters concerning the Association. It shall appoint its President and its officers and shall adopt its own rules of procedure.

The Parliamentary Conference shall be prepared by a Joint Committee set up on a basis of parity.

Article 51. (1) Disputes concerning the interpretation or the application of the present Convention which might arise between one Member State, several Member States or the Community on the one hand, and one or more Associated States on the other, shall be submitted by one of the parties to the Association Council which shall seek an amicable settlement at its next meeting. If this cannot be achieved and if the parties to the dispute fail to agree upon an appropriate solution, the dispute shall, at the request of the earliest petitioner, be submitted to the Court of Arbitration of the Association.

(2) The Court of Arbitration shall be composed of five members: a President who shall be appointed by the Association Council and four judges from among persons whose independence and competence can be fully guaranteed. The judges shall be appointed by the Association Council within three months after the entry into force of the Convention and for duration thereof. Two of the judges shall be appointed by the Council of the European Economic Community and the other two by the Associated States. For each judge, following the same procedure, the Association Council shall appoint a deputy who shall sit in the event of the accredited judge being unable to do so.

(3) The Court of Arbitration shall act by majority vote.

(4) The decisions of the Court of Arbitration shall be binding on the parties to the dispute who shall be under the obligation to take all necessary measures to carry them out.

(5) Within three months after the judges are appointed, the Association Council shall lay down the Statute of the Court of Arbitration, on a proposal of that Court.

(6) The Court of Arbitration shall adopt its rules of procedure within the same period.

Article 52. The Association Council may make any useful recommendation for the purpose of facilitating contacts between the Community and the representatives of the various trades and professions of the Associated States.

Article 53. The administrative expenses of the Institutions of the

Association shall be defrayed in accordance with the terms set out in Protocol No. 6 annexed to this Convention.

TITLE V. GENERAL AND FINAL PROVISIONS

Article 54. No treaties, conventions, agreements or arrangements of whatever form or nature between one or more Member States and one or more Associated States shall preclude the implementation of the provisions of this Convention.

Article 55. This Convention shall apply to the European territory of the Member States of the Community on the one hand, and to the territory of the Associated States on the other.

The First Title of this Convention shall also apply to the relations between the French Overseas Territories and the Associated States.

Article 56. As far as the Community is concerned, this Convention shall be validly concluded by a decision of the Council of the Community taken in conformity with the provisions of the Treaty and notified to the Parties. It shall be ratified by the Signatory States in conformity with their respective constitutional requirements.

The instruments of ratification and the act of notification of the conclusion of the Convention shall be deposited with the Secretariat of the Councils of the European Communities, who shall give notice thereof to the Signatory States.

Article 57. (1) This Convention shall enter into force on the first day of the month following the date on which the instruments of ratification of the Member States and of at least fifteen of the Associated States and the instrument notifying the conclusion of the Convention by the Community have been deposited.

(2) Any Associated State which has not ratified the Convention by the date of its entry into force as provided for in the previous paragraph, shall be able to proceed with this ratification only during the twelve months following such entry into force, unless before the expiry of this period it gives notice to the Association Council of its intention to ratify the Convention not later than six months after this period, and on condition that it deposits its instruments of ratification within the same time limit.

(3) As regards those States which have not ratified the Convention by the date of its entry into force as laid down in paragraph 1, the provisions of the Convention shall become applicable on the first day of the month following the deposit of their respective instruments of ratification.

Signatory States who ratify the Convention in accordance with the terms of paragraph 2 shall recognize the validity of all measures taken in implementation of the said Convention between the date of its entry into force and the date when its provisions become applicable to them. Without prejudice to any delay which might be granted to them by the Association Council, they shall, not later than six months after depositing their instruments of ratification, carry out all the obligations which devolve upon them under the terms of this Convention or of implementing decisions adopted by the Association Council.

(4) The rules of procedure of the organs of the Association shall lay down if and under what conditions the representatives of Signatory States which, on the date of entry into force of the Convention, have not yet ratified it, shall sit in the organs of the Association as observers. The arrangements thus adopted shall only be effective until the date on which the Convention becomes applicable to these States; in any case, they shall cease to apply on the date on which, according to the terms of paragraph 2 above, the State concerned shall no longer be able to proceed with the ratification of the Convention.

Article 58. (1) The Association Council shall be informed of any request made by a State for accession to or association with the Community.

(2) There shall be consultations within the Association Council on any request for association with the Community made by a State which has an economic structure and production comparable to those of the Associated States if the Community, after examining the said request, has laid it before the Association Council.

(3) The agreement of association between the Community and any State covered by the previous paragraph may provide for the accession of that State to the present Convention. That State shall then enjoy the same rights and be subject to the

same obligations as the Associated States. Provided always that the agreement which associates it with the Community may determine the date on which certain of these rights and obligations shall become applicable to it.

Such accession shall not adversely affect the advantages accruing to the Associated States which are signatories to this Convention from the provisions relating to financial and technical co-operation.

Article 59. This Convention shall be concluded for a period of five years from the date of its entry into force.

Article 60. One year before the expiry of this Convention, the Contracting Parties shall examine the provisions which might be made for a further period.

The Association Council shall if necessary take any transitional measures required until the new Convention enters into force.

Article 61. The Community and the Member States shall undertake the obligations set out in Articles 2, 5 and 11 of the Convention with respect to Associated States which, on the grounds of international obligations applying at the time of the entry into force of the Treaty establishing the European Economic Community and subjecting them to a particular customs treatment, may consider themselves not yet able to offer the Community the reciprocity provided for by Article 3, paragraph 2 of the Convention.

The Contracting Parties concerned shall re-examine the situation not later than three years after the entry into force of the Convention.

Article 62. This Convention may be denounced by the Community in respect of any Associated State and by any Associated State in respect of the Community by means of six months' notice.

Article 63. The Protocols annexed to this Convention shall form an integral part thereof.

Article 64. The present Convention, drawn up in a single original in the German, French, Italian and Dutch languages, each of these texts being equally authentic, shall be deposited in the archives of the Secretariat of the Councils of the European Communities which shall transmit a certified copy to the Government of each of the Signatory States.

In witness whereof, the undersigned Plenipotentiaries have affixed their signatures below this Convention.

Done at Yaoundé on the twentieth day of July in the year one thousand nine hundred and sixty-three.

PART IV

The Community and the Anglo-Saxon World

DOCUMENT 18. EXTRACTS FROM THE STATEMENT MADE BY THE RT. HONOURABLE EDWARD HEATH, M.P., LORD PRIVY SEAL, LEADER OF THE UNITED KINGDOM DELEGATION, AT THE MEETING IN PARIS ON 10 OCTOBER 1961, BETWEEN THE MEMBER GOVERNMENTS OF THE EUROPEAN ECONOMIC COMMUNITY AND HER MAJESTY'S GOVERNMENT IN THE UNITED KINGDOM OF GREAT BRITAIN AND NORTHERN IRELAND

2. I am deeply conscious of the importance of this occasion and of the work on which we are embarking together. There can be no doubt that the success or failure of these discussions will determine the future shape of Europe. They will affect profoundly the way of life, the political thought and even the character of each one of our peoples. Her Majesty's Government in the United Kingdom have asked me to set before you today, in clear and comprehensive terms, the view they take of this enterprise and to emphasize the importance which they attach to its success.

3. The British Government and the British people have been through a searching debate during the last few years on the subject of their relations with Europe. The result of the debate has been our present application. It was a decision arrived at, not on any narrow or short-term grounds, but as a result of a thorough assessment over a considerable period of the needs of our own country, of Europe and of the Free World as a whole. We recognize it as a great decision, a turning point in our history, and we take it in all seriousness. In saying that we wish to join the EEC, we mean that we desire to become full, wholehearted and active members of the European Com-

munity in its widest sense and to go forward with you in the building of a new Europe.

4. Perhaps you will allow me to underline some of the considerations which have determined our course of action. In the first place, ever since the end of the war, we in Britain have had a strong desire to play a full part in the development of European institutions. We, no less than any other European people, were moved by the enthusiasms which gave birth to the Brussels Treaty, the Council of Europe, the OEEC, the Western European Union and the North Atlantic Treaty. These organizations, based on the general principle of co-operation between sovereign states, played an important role in developing amongst us all the practice of working together. They gave us that knowledge of one another's institutions, practices and modes of thought, which is the necessary foundation for common action. Many are the tables round which we have all sat—round which our officials and experts have sat—during the last fifteen years, creating bit by bit the habit of international co-operation and joint action on which our present friendships and understandings are based.

5. Then there came a point when you decided to move a stride ahead towards a more organic type of unity; and my country, though understanding this move, did not then feel able to take part in it. It is true to say, however, that it was never agreeable to us to find that we were no longer running with the stream towards European unity. There were reasons for it and we knew them; but we did not feel comfortable to be outside. Nor, I believe, did you feel entirely comfortable to see us outside. One of our main purposes today is to discover afresh the inspiration and the stimulus of working together in a new effort of political and economic construction.

6. The second consideration has been the increasing realization that, in a world where political and economic power is becoming concentrated to such a great extent, a larger European unity has become essential. Faced with the threats which we can all see, Europe must unite or perish. The United Kingdom, being part of Europe, must not stand aside. You may say that we have been slow to see the logic of this. But all who are familiar with our history will understand that the decision was not an easy one. We had to weigh it long and carefully.

7. In particular, we had to think very deeply about the effect on the Commonwealth of so important a development in United Kingdom policy. I hope you will agree with me that the Commonwealth makes an essential contribution to the strength and stability of the world, and that sound economic foundations and prospects of development go hand in hand with this. We believe that it is in the interests of all of us round this table that nothing should be done which would be likely to damage the essential interests of its Member Countries. Some people in the United Kingdom have been inclined to wonder whether membership of the Community could in fact be reconciled with membership of the Commonwealth. The task of reconciliation is complex, but we are confident that solutions can be found to Commonwealth problems fully compatible with the substance and the spirit of the Treaty of Rome.

8. The third factor determining our decision has been the remarkable success of your Community and the strides which you have made towards unity in both political and economic fields. This has been in many ways an object lesson. You have shown what can be done in a Community comprising a group of countries with a will to work closely together. Our wish is to take part with you in this bold and imaginative venture; to unite our efforts with yours; and to join in promoting, through the EEC the fullest possible measure of European unity.

9. Against the background I have described you will, I hope, recognize that the United Kingdom has taken a momentous and carefully weighed decision. We are convinced that our destiny is intimately linked with yours. The decision we have taken reflects that conviction. Public opinion in my country has moved a long way during the last few years and more especially during the last twelve months. I think that opinion in the Member Countries of the Community has likewise developed. In particular I have noticed a growing understanding of the importance of the Commonwealth, and of the problems which would be created for Commonwealth countries by our entry into the Community. I have no doubt that, as all these issues continue to be debated, they will be understood with increasing clarity.

10. Our application has been made in a positive spirit. I

hope that what I now have to say will amply demonstrate our determination to bring these negotiations to a successful conclusion.

THE TREATY OF ROME

11. Her Majesty's Government are ready to subscribe fully to the aims which you have set yourselves. In particular, we accept without qualification the objectives laid down in Articles 2 and 3 of the Treaty of Rome, including the elimination of internal tariffs, a common customs tariff, a common commercial policy, and a common agricultural policy.

12. We are ready to accept, and to play our full part in, the institutions established under Article 4 and other Articles of the Treaty.

13. So far as we can judge at this stage, we see no need for any amendments to the text of the Treaty, except of course in those Articles where adaptations are plainly required consequent upon the admission of a new Member. We think it should be possible to deal with our special problems by means of protocols. This would be very much in line with the procedure adopted for dealing with the special problems of the original signatories when the Treaty was drafted.

14. In addition to the major problems mentioned in our application, about which I will speak later, there will, of course, be other subjects arising from various Articles of the Treaty which we should like to discuss with you. Since the Treaty came into force decisions, recommendations, directives, and regulations have been adopted. How far these measures can be applied to the United Kingdom as they stand should, I suggest, be a matter for joint examination. In some cases this could wait until after our accession to the Treaty. On other, more vital, matters either you or we would doubtless wish to have a measure of mutual understanding before our accession.

15. The sort of things I have particularly in mind mostly concern what one might call the ancillary provisions of the Treaty. I will give you a few examples. Our system of social security and social benefits is different from the systems in force in your own countries; this raises certain problems which

154

we would like to discuss with you. Another example is the question of monopolies and restrictive practices: we have legislation which has the same objectives as those of the relevant Articles of the Treaty of Rome, but which provides for a procedure different in detail from that which the Treaty envisages. A third example lies in the field of establishment and services. Although we take pride in the fact that our legislation involves relatively little discrimination against foreign nationals, we may nevertheless need additional time to bring our law and practice into line with whatever programme there may be for the Community. Fourthly, we shall wish to discuss with you how our exchange control practice could be harmonized with the 'First Directive' on capital movements.

16. None of these matters for joint examination should be the cause of major difficulty. We are anxious that our accession to the Treaty should not tend to slow up the progress towards harmonization. We should be happy, if that were your general wish, to arrange for technical discussions on these matters to take place with your experts simultaneously with the negotiations on the problems of Commonwealth trade and United Kingdom agriculture.

17. Now I turn to a central feature of the European Economic Community—the common external tariff. We see no need to ask you for a re-negotiation, item by item, of the existing common external tariff of the Community. We assume that some adjustments are a necessary consequence of the admission of a new Member. It seems to us that, if the common external tariff of the enlarged Community is to be broadly acceptable to GATT and to third countries, it cannot remain at precisely the level of the existing one. At the same time we recognize that the negotiation of the present common external tariff was a long and difficult process, and that you might not wish to begin detailed negotiations all over again. We are moreover anxious that the process of adjustment should raise the minimum of practical problems. We think it important, in this and in other fields, to simplify the task before us.

18. We are therefore ready—and I hope that this simple solution may be agreeable to all of you—to accept the structure of the present EEC tariff as the basis of the common tariff of the enlarged Community. In these circumstances we think

that the necessary lowering of tariff levels might be achieved by making a linear cut in the common tariff as it stands today. We would suggest that this might be of the order of 20 per cent, a figure which the Community have considered in another context. No doubt both you and we would wish to single out some items for special treatment. I can assure you that our own list will not be long.

19. We are also ready, once we enter the Community, to make, in a single operation, the same cuts in tariffs on trade between Member States as you will have yourselves made by that date. In addition we are prepared to move our most favoured nation tariff towards the new common tariff by a step equivalent to that which you have already taken. This would be a considerable leap forward; but it is one which we are ready to make in the interests of the Community as a whole.

20. So far I have spoken entirely about the European Economic Community. But we recognize that the unity of the Six goes beyond the EEC. I should like now to say something about our attitude towards the European Coal and Steel Community, Euratom and the Bonn Declaration of the 18th of July.

21. As regards the ECSC and Euratom, we shall be prepared, as I told the House of Commons during the debate on the 3rd of August, to enter into negotiations with you, at the appropriate moment, with a view to joining these two Communities when we join the EEC.

22. We have followed with close interest your progress towards greater unity in fields other than those covered by the three existing Communities. The latest public statement of your position in these matters was the Declaration issued by the Heads of State and of Government at their meeting in Bonn on the 18th of July. We fully share the aims and objectives, political and otherwise, of those who drew up this Declaration, and we shall be anxious, once we are members of the Community, to work with you in a positive spirit to reinforce the unity which you have already achieved. That indeed animates our whole approach. The more that we, the United Kingdom, can contribute to the unifying process of this great European Community, the more we shall feel that we are

joining the historic enterprise which the genius of the European peoples has launched.

23. I have heard it suggested that, if we join the Community, it will be our aim to slow down the pace of its development. I beg you to believe that this is not so. The concrete proposals I have put forward in the field of tariffs show that, far from wishing to slow up the progress of the EEC, we are determined to take the necessary action in this sphere to enable us to move at the same pace as you yourselves and in step with you. I do not imagine that any of us would care to hazard a guess as to the form which the Community may take in fifteen or twenty years' time. But I am convinced that we share the same essential interests and that the habit of working closely together, which you have learned over the past four years, and in which we should now like to join, will mean, not the slowing down of this process, but a continued advance and the development of closer unity.

THREE MAJOR PROBLEMS

24. I will now turn to the three major problems posed by the particular circumstances of the United Kingdom for which we have to seek solutions together. As you all know, these problems are those of Commonwealth trade, of United Kingdom agriculture, and of the arrangements which could be made for our partners in the European Free Trade Association.

25. I wish to make it clear that we are not seeking a privileged position for the United Kingdom. We fully recognize that the solutions to be worked out must be compatible with, and not disruptive of, the Common Market. In drafting the Treaty the original signatories were faced with a large number of special difficulties in entering the Community. In one way or another solutions were found for all of them. I do not think that the problems for which we would wish to negotiate special arrangements differ in principle from those which you yourselves faced in the earlier negotiations. But they obviously differ in magnitude. We recognize that they will only be solved by a joint effort based on good will and on a mutual understanding of what all of us are trying to achieve, politically as well as economically.

THE COMMONWEALTH

26. We believe that you share our view of the value of the Commonwealth, not only to the United Kingdom but also to yourselves and to the whole Free World. The Commonwealth is an association of peoples stretching into every continent and comprising many races. It is a great force in the world for the promotion of ideals and purposes which are widely shared in Europe. Its origins are based in history, in the fact that the members of the Commonwealth were parts of the British Empire, and much of its strength lies in the perpetuation of the links that were then formed. I should be misleading you if I failed to say how deeply the British people feel about this association. That, I am sure, is a sentiment which the Members of the Community will fully understand.

27. Commonwealth trade is one of the strongest elements in maintaining the Commonwealth association. It would be a tragedy if our entry into the Community forced other members of the Commonwealth to change their whole pattern of trade and consequently perhaps their political orientation. I do not think that such a development would be in your interests any more than in ours. Nor, looking at it now from the point of view of a potential member of the Community, would any of us wish the Community to be met with the hostility which would flow from a large group of countries strung across the world if they were to feel that their interests had suffered at our hands.

28. The economies of most Commonwealth countries have been built up on the basis of supplying the British market, which has traditionally imported their produce duty free and often on preferential terms. In the last few decades the majority of them have sought to enlarge both the variety of their production and the range of their markets. But the British market is still of great importance to the economies of most Commonwealth countries.

29. I am sure that you will understand that Britain could not join the EEC under conditions in which this trade connection was cut with grave loss and even ruin for some of the Commonwealth countries. For our remaining Dependent Territories we have a special and direct responsibility.

30. The problem of Commonwealth trade has analogies in the problems which faced you when you were negotiating the Treaty of Rome. Your problems concerned a considerable number of countries which were in varying constitutional relationships with Members of the Community. The total volume of trade affected was large. Your problems were dealt with, either in the Treaty or in its accompanying Protocols, without damage to the interests of the countries concerned, and in some cases with considerable advantage to them. It is a striking fact, and very relevant to the Commonwealth problem, that in no case was a tariff imposed on trade where one had not been in force before the Treaty was signed. Broadly speaking, it appears to us that two alternative solutions were applied according to the different circumstances. For some countries— Morocco and Tunisia for example—the problem was solved by maintaining, unimpaired by the Treaty, their right of access to the market of the country with which they were associated. For others, who became Associated Overseas Countries or Territories, not only was their right of access to their metropolitan country preserved, but they gained a preferential position for their products in the Common Market as a whole.

31. We recognize that the problem of Commonwealth trade is more extensive in scale and range than these earlier problems. The differences should not be exaggerated. Thirty-six per cent of our imports come from the Commonwealth; but I think I am correct in saying that over 20 per cent of metropolitan France's imports come from territories having a special relationship with her. Be that as it may, the trade is of very great importance to the Commonwealth countries concerned. For example, among the dependent or newly independent countries, Mauritius sends 82 per cent of her exports to the United Kingdom; Sierra Leone 70 per cent; and Nigeria 51 per cent. Of the older Commonwealth countries, New Zealand is also heavily dependent on the United Kingdom market, sending 56 per cent of her exports to us. The proportions of their exports which Australia, India and Ceylon send to the United Kingdom are of the order of 30 per cent.

32. On the assumption that there is general recognition of the need to devise satisfactory arrangements to protect vital

interests of Commonwealth countries, and with this background in mind, I think it would be helpful to suggest in more detail how the problem might be split up into its different components, and how each of these might be treated . . .

UNITED KINGDOM AGRICULTURE

47. I now turn to the question of United Kingdom agriculture. Here, let me say at once, we start from common ground. The agricultural objectives of the Treaty of Rome are in line with the objectives of our own agricultural policy. We, like you, are fully committed to the maintenance of a stable, efficient and prosperous agriculture. The Treaty of Rome aims at increasing agricultural productivity, a fair standard of living for the agricultural population, stable markets, regular supplies, and reasonable prices and supplies to consumers. These objectives command our wholehearted support. Moreover, we are now prepared to take the major step of participating with you in a common agricultural policy and in developing a common organization of agricultural markets. We fully accept that the Common Market must extend to agriculture and trade in agricultural products.

48. This, however, poses big problems for us. Our system of support, except for horticultural produce, relies mainly on Exchequer payments to ensure the maintenance of a satisfactory standard of living for our farmers. Our tariffs on foodstuffs are low and a large proportion of our supplies, particularly those from the Commonwealth, enter our market free of duty. We make very little use of import restrictions. Broadly speaking, we buy our food at world free market prices. Our people are therefore accustomed to low prices for food. Their tastes are related to a traditional pattern of food supplies.

49. At the same time our farmers have guaranteed prices for all their principal products. These guarantees are provided by means of Exchequer payments which make up the difference between the average price realized by farmers on the market and the guaranteed price determined by the Government. In addition we make direct farming grants designed to encourage improved farming methods and to raise the general efficiency of the industry. The level of the guaranteed prices, and of the

direct farming grants, is settled annually by the Government after consultation with the producers' representatives. We have legislation which sets definite limits to the amount of the reductions which may be made from one year to the next, both in the general level of support and in the guaranteed prices for individual commodities. The United Kingdom Government have pledged themselves to make no change in these statutory limits during the lifetime of the present Parliament which can continue until October 1964.

50. Our farmers are thus assured of reasonable stability of income. Furthermore the annual review of the guarantees provides the opportunity for a careful examination of the economic condition and prospects of the industry. This annual review is a key feature of our system. It enables us to look, not only at the prices of individual commodities, but at all the main factors affecting the industry's prosperity. The review is conducted on the basis of statistics which have been discussed fully with the farmers' representatives. We assess the extent of changes in farmers' costs since the last review and make assumptions about the gain from increasing efficiency. In order to discount the effects of particular weather conditions, we look at the level of farmers' incomes not only as they have actually developed but as they would have done under normal weather conditions. We also study the trend of production of individual commodities, the likely movement of imports, the prospective course of demand, and the way in which market prices can be expected to develop in the coming year. We take account of all these factors, together with the cost of Exchequer support, in determining the level of guaranteed prices and direct farming grants. We are also able to take account of the effects of our policy on our trade relations with the Commonwealth and with other overseas suppliers.

51. The annual review is therefore a comprehensive examination of the agricultural situation, and the United Kingdom Government are able to relate their decisions on the level of the guarantees to the national economic situation and to the prospects for the farming community. The Government and the farmers' representatives do not always agree on the measures to be taken. But the farmers have the assurance that their case will be fully examined in all its aspects and that the Govern-

ment's decisions are not taken without due regard to their interests. They are protected, not only by the legislation about the fixing of guarantees, but also by this institutional machinery which ensures a thorough examination of the effects of Government policy on their financial position. The Government can in fact judge, year by year, whether they are carrying out their satisfactory standard of living for the farming community.

52. The method of support which characterizes our present system is very different from the methods to which you are accustomed. It has been developed to meet our particular situation, and it is one in which our farmers have come to place great faith. They value especially the stability it secures, the sound basis it provides for planning ahead, and the fact that the system of annual reviews ensures that changes are made gradually and with due regard to their effects on the level of farming incomes. I need not emphasize the advantage which the consumer enjoys under our system and which in turn helps the producer, since low food prices encourage demand. In moving towards your methods of support we should have to introduce great changes affecting both producers and consumers. But provided we can see that in future—with the new methods decided upon—we are able to maintain the stability and living standards that we have established for our farmers, I believe that the problems raised by the differences in our present methods are in no way insuperable.

53. I am sure that the pooling of ideas and experience will have fruitful results; indeed, some features of our arrangements may prove attractive to you. Our object will be to consider with you how the essential interests of our farmers can be effectively safeguarded within the framework of the Treaty of Rome and in consonance with the objectives of the common agricultural policy.

54. We are encouraged by the recognition which the Treaty itself gives to the importance of ensuring that changes in agriculture are brought about gradually. If the necessary changes in the United Kingdom are to be introduced without harmful effects to our agricultural economy, or indeed to our economy as a whole, the period allowed must be long enough to give our farmers time to adjust to new conditions and to permit increases in food prices to the consumer to take place

gradually. We start, as I have said, with a system of support very different from yours, and one that has been developed to meet our particular situation. Perhaps one or two figures will help to bring out the importance of our support system in relation to the standard of living of our farmers. The agricultural industry's total receipts amount to about £1,600 million a year. Its net income is about £360 million. The total Exchequer payments to the industry is of the order of £270 million a year, or three-quarters of the industry's net income. We should thus be facing more fundamental changes in our system than you have to face and we should be joining the Community some years later. I feel sure that you will agree that the transitional arrangements for the United Kingdom should take account of these circumstances, and that the conditions under which our agriculture is brought within the common policy should not be more onerous than those which were open to you when the Treaty of Rome entered into force. On this basis the transitional arrangements for the United Kingdom could, where necessary, continue for a period of between twelve and fifteen years from when we join. Timing will, of course, differ for different commodities. For some we should certainly hope that a shorter period would be sufficient. In general we should wish to keep pace with you as far as we are able.

EFTA

58. I should next like to consider the position of the countries associated with the United Kingdom in the European Free Trade Association. It has long been our view that the present division of Western Europe into two economic groups—a division which in our opinion has political as well as economic dangers—should be brought to an end. We believe that the other members of EFTA, including the neutral countries, have a significant part to play, and that it would be wrong from the political as well as the economic point of view, if they were excluded. In recent months we and our EFTA partners have considered this problem very carefully. As you will know from the statement issued by the EFTA Council on 31st of July, we concluded that each member of EFTA should examine the possibility of entering into a direct relationship with the Community.

59. The United Kingdom and Denmark have already applied for full membership. We were delighted to hear of your decision to open negotiations with the Danish Government later this month. Some members of EFTA consider that for political reasons they cannot apply for full membership. We believe that this should not be allowed to prevent them finding an appropriate relationship with the Community. At the EFTA Council Meeting in London last June we agreed with our EFTA partners to maintain the Association—and here I quote from the Communiqué—'until satisfactory arrangements have been worked out . . . to meet the various legitimate interests of all members of EFTA, and thus enable them all to participate from the same date in an integrated European market'. Her Majesty's Government earnestly trust that, when the other EFTA countries have explained where they stand, it will be possible to agree on ways and means of meeting their legitimate interests. I am sure you will appreciate that, given our obligations to our EFTA partners, we should not ourselves be able to join the Community until this had been done.

60. There may in the past have been some misunderstanding of our views about arrangements for the EFTA countries. At the risk of some repetition I would like to make them perfectly clear. We hope to see an enlarged Community including ourselves and as many of our EFTA partners as may wish to become full Members. As to the remainder of the EFTA countries, we should like to see an association between each of them and the enlarged Community. If satisfactory arrangements could be made on these lines the wider trading area thus created would include, not only the Members of the enlarged Community, but also the remaining Members of EFTA, and, of course, Greece. EFTA itself would disappear. Contrary to what some people seem to have thought, therefore, there is no question of the United Kingdom seeking to maintain for itself a trading relationship with its present partners in EFTA in any way different from that which would be enjoyed by all other members of the enlarged Community . . .

CONCLUSION

65. All of us here have come a long way in the brief span of time since the end of the Second World War. The application

which we have made for membership of the Community, if it raises the difficulties which I have dealt with at some length, presents us all with a great opportunity for new advances together. We in the United Kingdom will regard the successful conclusion of these negotiations as a point of departure, not as the end of the road. The present dangers which confront the Free World generally, and Europe in particular, are an added spur to us in seeking a new step forward in European unity. On the one hand we have a situation in which—owing to the advent of so many new States—the old and experienced voices of Europe find themselves more and more in a minority in world councils. We also have the phenomenon of blocs and groupings forming amongst these new States for the purpose of furthering their interests and increasing their influence in the world. On the other hand, nearer home, we have the direct threat to the security and well-being of European peoples from Communist expansionism, and in particular the threat to Berlin which weighs so heavily upon us at the present time. Great European nations have heard themselves described as 'hostages'. I can imagine no better way of counteracting the anxieties to which these events give rise in all our countries than by making rapid and visible progress with the task which we are undertaking today. An early success in this would, I think, do more than anything else to restore confidence in the future. It would compel our adversaries to treat us all with new respect, and encourage all who believe in the future of free peoples.

DOCUMENT 19. EXTRACTS FROM PRESIDENT KENNEDY'S 'DECLARA-TION OF INTERDEPENDENCE', PHILADELPHIA, 4 JULY 1962

You and I are the executors of the testament handed down by those who gathered in this historic hall 186 years ago today. For they gathered . . . to assert the independence of free states in place of colonies, and to commit to that goal their fortunes and their sacred honour . . . For 186 years, this doctrine of national independence has shaken the globe.

There are those struggling to eke out a bare existence in a barren land who have never heard of free enterprise but who cherish the idea of independence.

There are those who are grappling with overpowering problems of illiteracy and ill health and who are ill-equipped to hold free elections. But they are determined to hold fast to their national independence. Even those unwilling or unable to take part in any struggle between East and West are strongly on the side of their own national independence.

If there is a single issue in the world which divides the world it is independence—the independence of Berlin, or Laos, or Vietnam; the longing for independence behind the Iron Curtain, the peaceful transition to independence in those newly emerging areas whose troubles some hope to exploit.

The theory of independence is as old as man himself, and it was not invented in this hall. But it was in this hall that the theory became a practice; that the word went out to all, in Thomas Jefferson's phrase—'that the God who gave us life gave us liberty at the same time.' . . .

As apt and applicable as the Declaration of Independence is today, we would do well to honour that other historic document drafted in this hall, the Constitution of the United States.

For it stressed not independence, but interdependences; not the individual liberty of one, but the indivisible liberty of all. In most of the old colonial world the struggle for independence is coming to an end. Even in areas behind the curtain, that which Jefferson called 'the disease of liberty' still appears to be infectious.

With the passing of ancient empires, today less than two per cent of the world's population live in territories officially termed dependent. As this effort for independence, inspired by the American Declaration of Independence, now approaches a successful close, a great new effort for interdependence is transforming the world about us. And the spirit of that new effort is the same spirit which gave birth to the American Constitution.

That spirit is today most clearly seen across the Atlantic Ocean. The nations of Western Europe, long divided by feuds far more bitter than any which existed among the thirteen colonies, are today joining together, seeking, as our forefathers sought, to find freedom in diversity and unity from strength.

The United States looks on this vast new enterprise with

166

hope and admiration. We do not regard a strong and united Europe as a rival, but a partner. To aid its progress has been the basic object of our foreign policy for seventeen years.

We believe that a united Europe will be capable of playing a greater role in the common defence of responding more generously to the needs of poorer nations, of joining with the United States and others in lowering trade barriers, resolving problems of commerce and commodities and currency, and developing co-ordinated policies in all economic, political and diplomatic areas.

We see in such a Europe a partner with whom we can deal on a basis of full equality in all the great and burdensome tasks of building and defending a community of free nations.

It would be premature at this time to do more than indicate the high regard with which we view the formation of this partnership. The first order of business is for our European friends to go forward in forming the more perfect union which will some day make this partnership possible.

A great new edifice is not built overnight. It was eleven years from the Declaration of Independence to the writing of the Constitution. The construction of workable Federal institutions required still another generation.

The greatest works of our nation's founders lay not in documents and in declarations, but in creative, determined action. The building of the new house of Europe has followed the same practical purposeful course. Building the Atlantic partnership now will not be easily or cheaply finished.

But I will say here and now, on this Day of Independence, that the United States will be ready for a declaration of interdependence, that we will be prepared to discuss with a United Europe the ways and means of forming a concrete Atlantic partnership, a mutually beneficial partnership between the new union now emerging in Europe and the old American union founded here 175 years ago.

All this will not be completed in a year, but let the world know it is our goal.

In urging the adoption of the United States Constitution, Alexander Hamilton told his fellow New Yorkers 'to think continentally'. Today Americans must learn to think intercontinentally.

Acting on our own, by ourselves, we cannot establish justice throughout the world; we cannot insure its domestic tranquility, or provide for its common defence, or promote its general welfare, or secure the blessings of liberty to ourselves and our posterity. But joined with other free nations, we can do all this and more.

We can assist the developing nations to throw off the yoke of poverty. We can balance our world-wide trade and payments at the highest possible level of growth. We can mount a deterrent powerful enough to deter any aggression. And ultimately we can help to achieve a world of law and free choice, banishing the world of war and coercion.

For the Atlantic partnership of which I speak would not look inward only, preoccupied with its own welfare and advancement. It must look outward to co-operate with all nations in meeting their common concerns. It would serve as a nucleus for the eventual union of all free men—those who are now free and those who are vowing that some day they will be free . . .

And for the support of this Declaration, with a firm reliance on the protection of Divine Providence, we mutually pledge to each other our Lives, our Fortunes and our sacred Honour.'

DOCUMENT 20. LABOUR AND THE COMMON MARKET. STATEMENT BY THE NATIONAL EXECUTIVE COMMITTEE, 29 SEPTEMBER 1962

I. LABOUR'S APPROACH

The Labour Party regards the European Community as a great and imaginative conception. It believes that the coming together of the six nations which have in the past so often been torn by war and economic rivalry is, in the context of Western Europe, a step of great significance. It is aware that the influence of this new Community on the world will grow and that it will be able to play—for good or for ill—a far larger part in the shaping of events in the 1960s and the 1970s than its individual member states could hope to play alone.

It is these considerations, together with the influence that Britain as a member could exercise upon the community—and not the uncertain balance of economic advantage—that constitute the real case for Britain's entry.

The Labour Party, however, is also aware that membership

of the Common Market would involve commitments to the nations of the Six which, in their scope and depth, go far beyond our relationships with any other group of nations. For the central purpose of the Common Market is not just the removal of trade barriers between its member states, but the conscious merging of their separate national economies into a single unit. Within this single Community the power of national governments over commercial, industrial, financial, agricultural, fiscal and social policies will progressively wither away. In their place, common policies, arrived at by majority decisions, will emerge.

Moreover the Rome Treaty is itself only one expression of the will of the Six to closer political unity. The aim is to build on the foundations of the Common Market a single political Community, with a Common Parliament and, eventually, a Common Government. Powerful and ardent voices have indeed long urged the creation of a West European federal state.

For Britain, such wide commitments present special and serious difficulties. Full membership of the Common Market is limited to European states. Although there is provision for associated status for some territories, many important members of the Commonwealth will be totally excluded. Moreover our situation is not the same as that of the other countries of the Community. While our histories have certainly overlapped, they have also diverged, and this has shaped our separate institutions and policies. Our connections and interests, both political and economic, lie as much outside Europe as within it.

Membership of the Common Market could, therefore, decisively change our political and economic relations with the rest of the world. Unlike the Six, Britain is the centre and founder member of a much larger and still more important group, the Commonwealth. As such we have access to the largest single trading area in the world and political influence within a world-wide, multi-racial association of 700 million people.

Finally, although the unification of Western Europe is in itself a great historic objective, it has to be considered in the light of the effect it has on the two transcendent issues of our times: the cold war, with its immense threat of global destruction, and the ever increasing division of the world into the affluent nations of Europe and North America and the poverty-stricken nations elsewhere.

If by joining the Common Market we could mobilize the economic resources of Europe to help the underdeveloped nations of the world and to promote the cause of world peace by ensuring more creative and liberal policies in Europe, then, the case would indeed be strong.

If on the other hand our membership were to weaken the Commonwealth and the trade of the underdeveloped nations, lessen the chances of East-West agreement and reduce the influence that Britain could exert in world affairs, then the case against entry would be decisive.

The Labour Party has always looked upon the question of Britain's entry into the Common Market as a matter of balance, to be judged in the light of the long-term interests of the British people.

We could not take the view that whatever the circumstances, whatever the conditions, we should enter. Nor could we take the view that whatever the circumstances, whatever the conditions, we should stay out.

It was for these reasons that the National Executive Committee at the 1961 Annual Conference of the Labour Party refused to pass judgement on the abstract question of whether Britain should join the Common Market. Instead, it insisted that judgement should be deferred until the actual terms of entry were reasonably clear.

For it is the terms that really matter. At the 1961 Annual Conference, following a long debate, the Committee accepted a resolution in these terms:

'This Conference does not approve Britain's entry into the Common Market, unless guarantees protecting the position of British Agriculture and Horticulture, the EFTA countries and the Commonwealth are obtained, and Britain retains the power of using public ownership and economic planning as measures to ensure social progress within the United Kingdom.'

At the same time, the National Executive Committee made it clear that we would support Britain's entry if these terms were met. As Hugh Gaitskell put it in his broadcast of 8 May 1962:

'To go in on good terms would, I believe, be the best solution to this difficult problem. And let's hope we can get them. Not to go in would be a pity, but it would not be a catastrophe. To go in on bad terms, which really meant the end of the Commonwealth, would be a step which I think we would regret all our lives, and for which history would not forgive us.'

II. THE ESSENTIAL CONDITIONS

While deliberately refraining from hobbling the Brussels negotiations by laying down in advance a series of rigid and detailed terms, the Labour Party clearly stated the five broad conditions that would be required:

1. Strong and binding safeguards for the trade and other interests of our friends and partners in the Commonwealth.
2. Freedom as at present to pursue our own foreign policy.
3. Fulfilment of the Government's pledge to our associates in the European Free Trade Area.
4. The right to plan our own economy.
5. Guarantees to safeguard the position of British agriculture.

The acceptance by the Six of these five conditions—the arguments for which we outline below—would mean a conscious decision to liberalize their commercial policy and to become an outward-looking rather than an inward-looking community—one that recognizes, in deeds as well as words, that it has obligations not only to the 170 million people within the Common Market, but to the hundreds of millions outside.

The Commonwealth

The Commonwealth countries still export twice as much to Britain as they do to the whole of the Six put together. Britain in turn still exports to the Commonwealth more than twice as much is it does to the Common Market.

This pattern of trade, which accounts for roughly 40 per cent of our exports and imports, has been encouraged during the past thirty years by the system of Commonwealth Preference. Under these arrangements, Britain's tariffs do not apply to Commonwealth goods, which consequently enter Britain duty-free or on advantageous terms compared with the goods of other countries. British goods enjoy similar privileges in Commonwealth markets. While the size of these preferences has been reduced over the years, they are still substantial.

If Britain joined the Common Market as at present operated, we would abandon the whole system of Commonwealth preference, and in its place impose on Commonwealth goods the Common External Tariff of the Six. Thus, not only would Commonwealth countries exporting to Britain lose their preferential entry into the British market, but they would be actively discriminated against—while German, Italian, French and other European exports would enter the British market duty-free.

On Commonwealth foodstuffs, a special and crippling version of the Common External Tariff—the so-called Import Levies —is to be imposed. Whatever the efficiency of Commonwealth food producers the imposition of this system will ensure that they cannot effectively compete against European food producers inside the Community.

We cannot accept that such injurious arrangements should be inflicted on Commonwealth countries. Nor can we forget that whereas living standards in Europe are, measured by world standards, high, those of many of our Commonwealth partners in Asia, Africa and the Caribbean are desperately low.

With these points in mind the Labour Party has insisted that firm arrangements should be made to safeguard trade between Britain and the rest of the Commonwealth. Failure to do this could bring grave damage to such countries as India, Pakistan and New Zealand, the severance of the economic ties that today bind the Commonwealth, and a drastic weakening of its political cohesion.

Foreign Policy

In economic and social policies the Rome Treaty already allows for a substantial amount of supranational decision-making through the instrument of the Commission and the machinery of qualified majority voting.

We should be unwise to disregard the very real likelihood that in the attempt to achieve closer political union this system will be extended to foreign policy and defence.

No socialist will cling to national sovereignty for its own

sake. But Britain has special relations with many countries outside Europe—particularly in the Commonwealth. These relations would be imperilled if we were to accept majority decisions taken within the European Community in this field. Moreover, on such crucial questions as Berlin, disengagement, and support for the UN, an independent British voice is essential. For these reasons we believe that it is right to insist that Britain must retain full freedom of action in foreign policy.

EFTA

Three years ago, when the negotiations for a wider European trade association broke down, Norway, Denmark, Sweden, Switzerland, Portugal and Austria joined Britain in forming the European Free Trade Area.

Before applying for entry to the Common Market the United Kingdom Government made a solemn pledge to its EFTA partners that it would maintain the Association 'until satisfactory arrangements have been worked out . . . to meet the various legitimate interest of all members of EFTA, and thus enable them all to participate from the same date in an integrated European Market'.

This pledge must be honoured. In particular we cannot accept that Sweden, Switzerland and Austria should be denied associate membership on account of their neutrality. Indeed we regard the membership of the EFTA countries as a vital British interest.

Economic Planning

The prosperity of Britain rests far more on our ability to make intelligent use of our economic resources than it does on securing tariff-free access to the Six.

Some features of economic planning cannot be easily combined with membership of the Common Market. This is due in part to the *laissez-faire* assumptions underlying the Rome Treaty, in part to its basic aim of creating a single and competitive market.

Under the Rome Treaty, limitations are placed upon the powers of governments to intervene in their economies wherever such interventions are thought to distort competition or interfere with the free flow of trade, capital and labour.

While these limitations are not necessarily disadvantageous, they could in certain cases have dangerous consequences for Britain. Our balance of payments is weaker, our reserves smaller, the weight of our overseas debts vastly greater than is the case with many of the present members of the Community. Complete free trade with the Six and the free movement of capital out of Britain could well—and in the short run almost certainly will—intensify our balance-of-payments difficulties. If the power of the British Government to take corrective measures is limited, this could have grave consequences for full employment, for the strength of the currency and for our future prosperity. We must be sure, as the TUC has urged, that we can pursue policies necessary to secure full employment and the maintenance and improvement of our social services.

These are major considerations affecting the livelihood of millions of our fellow citizens. It is therefore only simple prudence to secure now either freedom of action for the British Government to tackle these problms or binding agreements with the Six on corrective action by the Community as a whole. For the same reason, the voting arrangements finally agreed on in the enlarged Community should be such as to ensure that in economic and social questions British interests cannot be over-ridden. This would be facilitated by the entry of the EFTA nations.

British Agriculture

Since the war the interests of British farmers, of Commonwealth producers and of consumers have been largely reconciled (though a great deal less effectively in recent years) by allowing the market price to be determined by low-cost imports and by safeguarding farm incomes through a system of agricultural planning, production grants and deficiency payments.

The food and agriculture policy of the Six is, however, very different. The aim of their policies in the past has been, and it is likely to continue to be, to make the area as a whole broadly self-sufficient. To this end, as we have already seen, Common Market farmers are to be protected from world exporters by a system of import levies, while consumers will continue to pay prices based on high-cost European production.

British farmers would lose the security of the existing system of protection and would be compelled to take, in return, a much less certain system whose operations would be determined not by the Ministry of Agriculture in London but by the Commission in Brussels.

We must insist that the negotiations should secure such modifications in the common agricultural policy as are necessary to give adequate security to British agriculture and horticulture.

III. THE ECONOMIC ARGUMENT

The Labour Party believes that these broad conditions constitute reasonable terms of entry. Only if such terms could be secured would it be right for Britain to enter the Common Market. But we emphasize that it would be the acceptance of these conditions which would tilt the balance in favour. There is no question of Britain being forced to go in. In particular we reject the widespread but false view that the economic advantages of membership are so great and the economic consequences of non-membership so disastrous that Britain has no choice but to accept whatever terms the Six may offer.

In our opinion the economic arguments for and against are evenly balanced.

The main arguments in favour are these. First, that as a member of the Community, Britain would share in a home market of over 200 million consumers. A market of such size would greatly stimulate production of low-cost mass-produced goods. Firms would be able to achieve all the economies of scale.

Secondly, in such a market it would be possible to have both very large firms and competition between them. As a result, a fresh wind would blow through British industry, bringing new ideas, accelerating change, encouraging a more competitive and enterprising economy.

Thirdly, trade between the members of the Common Market has grown very rapidly—more rapidly than in most other trade areas. If this continues in the years ahead, Britain as a member would greatly benefit.

Fourthly, if we do not go in we shall not only find it more difficult to compete with the Six in their own market, but also have to face stronger competition from them in world markets generally.

On the other hand, the contrary arguments are no less strong.

First, less than a fifth of our exports go to the Common Market. Any benefit we get from tariff-free access to the Six must be weighed against the losses of trade preferences that we now possess in Commonwealth and EFTA markets which absorb more than half of our exports.

Secondly, keener competition may well lead to the further concentration of industry, to monopoly and cartel agreements.

Thirdly, there is no evidence that a home market of 50 million consumers and a vast export market besides is incapable of providing our industries with all the advantages of large-scale manufacture.

Fourthly, it is wholly wrong to suggest that membership of the Common Market would transform Britain from a stagnant to a dynamic economy. The recent economic expansion of the Six owes little to the establishment of the Market.

Finally, our balance of payments will be adversely affected by higher food prices, by more foreign competition in the British market and by unrestricted capital movements.

Entry into the Common Market will not offer, in itself, an easy escape from our economic difficulties. The truth is that the growth of our economy and of our trade will owe far more to our own exertions, to the sensible planning of our economy, to reasonable restraint on incomes based on a fairer division of wealth, and to our ability to put investment and exports before home consumption, than to any consequence of our entry or non-entry into the Common Market.

DOCUMENT 21. EXTRACTS FROM MR. HUGH GAITSKELL'S SPEECH TO THE LABOUR PARTY CONFERENCE AT BRIGHTON, 3 OCTOBER 1962

... I turn to the political aspects. None of us surely would for one second deny the idealism implicit in the desire of European people in Germany and France and Italy and the Low Countries to join together, to get rid of the old enmities which have so often destroyed their countries and to be at one with each other. Let us recognize in particular the deep desire of the social democratic parties of the Six for this joining together. Let us pay tribute to them for this. It is no part of our business as socialists to seek to prevent countries who wish to join up from doing so.

And we must recognize this. The European Economic Community has come to stay. We are not passing judgement on that; it is not our affair. It may well be that political union will follow. It would be the height of folly to deny that therefore in the centre of Western Europe there will in all probability develop a new powerful combination, which may be a single state, and it would, of course, be absurd to question the immense impact that this can have upon world affairs.

Nor would I for one moment question the force of the argument so frequently put that it would be better, since this thing has come to stay, that we should go in now and influence it in the best way.

These are powerful arguments and we would be very foolish to brush them aside. But that is not to say that I, for one, am prepared to accept them as overriding everything else. They must be brought into the balance, but the balancing has not been completed.

And let me say this: Not all political unions are necessarily good in themselves. They must surely be judged by their consequences. If, for instance, it were proposed today that Britain should join a bloc of neutral countries, which I should be strongly against, as you know, and which I think a number of those in favour of our entry into the Common Market would be strongly against, they would not say this was a good thing. If it were proposed that we should join the USA, I do not think it would be universally popular or accepted as necessarily a contribution to world peace.

It all depends, does it not? For if we were presented today with a tremendous choice, whether to go into a world federation under a world government—which alone would finally prevent war—there is not one of us who would say No.

So let us have less of this talk of narrow nationalism. It is not a matter of just any union, it is a matter of what are the effects of the union. Is it an aggressive one? Is it damaging to others? Is it selfish? Is it inward-looking or is it internationally minded? Is it power-hungry or is it satisfied? Does it erect barriers as well as pull them down? All these questions have to be asked, if we are honest, before we can decide.

There is another point: I have already said that I understand and deeply sympathize with the people of France and of Germany in their desire to get rid of the conflicts which have so often broken out between them and which indeed are all too fresh in our minds. But I sometimes wonder whether the great problems of the world today are to be found in the unity or disunity of Western Europe. I would have said there were two problems outstanding above all others: the problem of peace and the problem of poverty; the problem of East-West relations that plagues us and the problem of the division of the world into the 'haves' and the 'have nots'.

I know some will say with great sincerity 'But we recognize that and we believe that by Britain going into Europe a great contribution can be made to these problems'. Maybe so, but it is for them to submit the proof. So far it is hard to be convinced. For although, of course, Europe has had a great and glorious civilization, although Europe can claim Goethe and Leonardo, Voltaire and Picasso, there have been evil features in European history, too—Hitler and Mussolini and today the attitude of some Europeans to the Congo problem, the attitude of at least one European government to the United Nations. You cannot say what this Europe will be; it has its two faces and we do not know as yet which is the one which will be dominant.

But here is another question we have to ask; what exactly is involved in the concept of political union? We hear a lot about it; we are told that the Economic Community is not just a customs union, that all who framed it saw it as a stepping stone towards political integration. We ought to be told what is meant by that, for if this be true our entry into the Common Market carries with it some very serious political obligations. But when you ask it is not easy to get a clear answer. When Mr. Macmillan speaks of belonging to a larger political unit what does he mean by 'belonging'? What are we supposed to be joining?

I can see only three possibilities outside the obligations that we accept specifically in the Treaty of Rome. It may mean that there is no obligation upon the Government of Britain to do more than talk, consult more frequently with the President of France and the Chancellor of Germany. I see no harm in these talks, but I am not terribly optimistic about what they will produce. It is hard to see this kind of thing producing, for example, any solution to the present attitude of President de Gaulle towards NATO; it is hard to see that it will change the views of Dr. Adenauer on Berlin; it is hard to see that out of this will emerge a satisfactory solution of the problems of preventing the spread of nuclear weapons. If indeed there is to be a major European state it is not going to be very easy in that kind of atmosphere and spirit to prevent that state having its own advanced independent store of nuclear weapons.

But what else? If it is not just talking what is it? The second possibility is majority decisions on political issues, just as we are to have majority decisions on economic issues. Do we want that? Well, I suppose you might say we would be able somehow or other to outvote those we disagree with. I would like to be very sure of that before I committed myself.

Then, of course, there is the idea and the ideal of Federal Europe. Now I know it will be said by some, 'Why bring up federation? It is not immediate, it is not imposed upon us, it may not happen'. But we would be foolish to deny, not to recognize and indeed sympathize with the desire of those who created the Economic Community for political federation. That is what they mean, that is what they are after when they admit freely that under the present constitution of EEC the Assembly has no powers except the very far-reaching, over-riding one, which they are most unlikely to use, of dismissing the Commission by a two-thirds majority. When it is pointed out that the Commission is a body which has powers but is not responsible or under anybody's control, what is the answer? The answer they give is: 'That is why we should set up a Federal Assembly with powers over them.' This is what they are arguing.

What does federation mean? It means that powers are taken from national governments and handed over to federal governments and to federal parliaments. It means—I repeat it—that if we go into this we are no more than a state (as it were) in the United States of Europe, such as Texas and California. They are remarkably friendly examples, you do not find every state as rich or having such good weather as those two! But I could take others: it would be the same as in Australia, where you have Western Australia, for example, and New South Wales. We should be like them. This is what it means; it does mean the end of Britain as an independent nation state. It may be a good thing or a bad thing but we must recognize that this is so . . .

DOCUMENT 22. EXTRACTS FROM A SPEECH BY MR. MICHAEL MASON, FORMER HIGH SHERIFF OF OXFORDSHIRE' MADE ON 13 DECEMBER 1962, AS REPORTED IN THE 'WITNEY GAZETTE'

The whole idea seems to be founded on calculated fundamental misconceptions.

The first is that Britain is done for, and cannot stand alone.

The second is that we are so poor we can't afford to fight or, apparently, even settle our own affairs without obeying the United States Government's wishes.

The third is that the countries of Europe are so much better than our own relatives that we should throw Canada, Australia, New Zealand and the rest of them overboard to become one blood with Germans, Frenchmen, Belgians, Dutchmen, Italians and Luxembourgers.

When I was born the South African Boer War was going on. Canadians, Australians and New Zealanders came as volunteers to fight on our side. In 1914–18 they did so in even greater measure. Not conscripts! Volunteers! In 1939–45 to a greater measure than ever. These men from what I prefer to call our Dominions (I don't like the word Commonwealth—makes me think of Cromwell) are of the same blood as ourselves. We talk the same language and think the same thoughts. We do not need interpreters when we deal with them. But now we are told we must throw them overboard.

So, to whom are we to ally ourselves, or, more probably subject ourselves? Let us take them in order.

France: Our enemy since England became England, not more than a 100 years after the Norman Conquest. A country which —as a little island lying just off her shore—we have invariably defeated. A country which folded up and surrendered in 1940 without firing a shot or dropping a bomb (de Gaulle appeared later). Once the mother of our civilization. Now the whorehouse of the world.

Germany: Only invented 100 years ago by Prince Bismarck. Has sought to devour the world ever since. Good soldiers but follow bad leaders. Make good American immigrants.

Holland: Only had a police-force as an army. More fifth-columnists than any other country. Honest and slow, and eat far too much. Shatteringly divided by religion. Duller than ditchwater.

Italy: Clever artisans, clever artists, good waiters, pretty women, rather greasy little men terribly anxious not to be hit or kicked. In times of strife they betray their allies and run from their enemies. Scum of the earth.

Belgium: A little buffer state, divided into two parts who hate each other's guts. Apparently invented so that while Germany is invading it other countries can get ready for war. A country with only two sources of strength: Antwerp and the Congo. The Congo was thrown upon the bonfire. Remains only the port of Antwerp and a little country of diminished merchants.

Luxembourg: Who the hell ever heard of it? It's about as big as Bedfordshire and not half as important . . .

Look at that gang of scarecrows: We are to put ourselves, cap in hand before them, asking for licence to be allowed to work and trade for our living, and to join them in a subordinate capacity as underlings in a Europe governed by Germany. England governed by some damned ex-Nazi Prussian Gauleiter, and our Queen perhaps an honorary Life-Vice-President—with no voice at all or even a place in the scene.

Some very intelligent people I know do believe in this Common Market. After all, the Prime Minister does. I've known him for 30 years, and never thought him a fool till the last year or so. But these 'little Britain must creep to safety under somebody's wing' crowd are none of them the people, like ourselves here in this room, who have their roots in the soil.

Big City merchants whose money employs thousands of men, but only know a few of their office staff by sight. They will probably cash in on it . . .

Let us all here, whose limbs were made in England, stick to our blood-relations in the world outside who still are proud to be subjects of our Queen, who think and talk like us, and have the same basic ideas of what is good and what is bad.

Our strength came from our being an island. Let us go on

being one. I wish the Atlantic Ocean was 10,000 miles wide and England in the middle of it.

DOCUMENT 23. EXTRACT FROM PRESIDENT DE GAULLE'S PRESS CONFERENCE HELD IN PARIS ON 14 JANUARY 1963

Question: Can you explicitly define France's position concerning the entry of Britain in the Common Market and the political evolution of Europe?

Answer: That is a clear question which I am going to try to answer clearly.

When we talk about economic matters, and even more when we are dealing with them, it is essential for what is said and what is done to conform to reality, for otherwise we end up in deadlocks and sometimes even ruined.

Concerning this very important question of the European Economic Community and also that of the possible membership of Great Britain, it is the facts which must be considered first. Sentiments, as favourable as they might be and as they are, cannot be put forward in opposition to the real factors of the problem. What are these factors?

The Treaty of Rome was concluded between six continental States. States which, economically speaking, are in short of the same nature. Whether in terms of their industrial or agricultural production, of their foreign trade, of their commercial customs and clients, or of their living and working conditions, there are many more similarities than differences between them. Moreover, they are adjacent, they interpenetrate, they are extensions of each other through their communications. The very fact of grouping them and linking them together in such a way that what they produce, buy, sell and consume, they produce, buy, sell and consume by preference within their own grouping thus conforms to reality.

It must be added, moreover, that from the standpoint of their economic development, their social progress and their technological capability they are, in short, in stride with each other and they are moving forward at more or less the same pace. Furthermore, it happens that there exists between them no kind of political grievance, no border disputes, no rivalry for domination or power. To the contrary, there is a feeling of solidarity between them, firstly owing to the awareness they have of together possessing an important part of the origins of our civilization, and also with regard to their security, because they are continental countries and they are confronted by the same single threat from one end of their territorial grouping to the other. Finally, they have a feeling of solidarity because not one of them is linked on the outside by any special political or military agreement.

Thus it has been psychologically and materially possible to organize an economic Community of the Six. Moreover, this was not without difficulty. When the Treaty of Rome was signed in 1957, it was after long discussions, and once concluded, so that something could be accomplished, it was necessary for us French to straighten ourselves out in the economic, financial and monetary domain. And this was done in 1959.

From that time on, the Community was workable in principle, but it was then necessary to implement the Treaty. Now this Treaty, which was quite specific and complete on the subject of industry, was not at all specific and complete on the subject of agriculture. And yet, it was essential for our country that this be settled.

For it is indeed quite obvious that agriculture is an essential element of our national activity as a whole. We cannot conceive of a common market in which French agriculture would not find outlets commensurate with its production, and we agree, moreover, that, among the Six, we are the country for which this necessity is the most imperative.

That is why last January, when consideration was being given to implementing the second stage of the Treaty, in other words, to a practical beginning of application, we were led to set the entry of agriculture into the Common Market as a formal condition.

This was finally accepted by our partners, but very complex and difficult arrangements were needed. And some of these arrangements are still being worked out. I will note in passing that, in this vast undertaking, all the decisions taken were taken by the Governments, for nowhere else is there any authority or responsibility. But I should say that, in order to prepare and clarify matters, the Brussels Commission worked in a highly objective and pertinent fashion.

Then Great Britain applied for membership in the Common Market. It did so after refusing earlier to participate in the community that was being built, and after then having created a free trade area with six other States, and finally—I can say this, the negotiations conducted for so long on this subject can be recalled—after having put some pressure on the Six in order to prevent the application of the Common Market from really getting started. Britain thus in its turn requested membership, but on its own conditions.

This undoubtedly raises for each of the six States and for England problems of a very great dimension.

England is, in effect, insular, maritime, linked through its trade, markets and food supply to very diverse and often very distant countries. Its activities are essentially industrial and commercial and only slightly agricultural. It has, throughout its work, very marked and original customs and traditions. In short, the nature, structure and economic context of England differ profoundly from those of the other States of the Continent.

What is to be done so that Britain, such as it lives, such as it produces and such as it trades, be incorporated into the Common Market such as it has been conceived and such as it functions?

For example, the means by which the people of Great Britain nourish themselves is in fact by importing foodstuffs purchased at low prices in the two Americas or in the former dominions, while still granting large subsidies to British farmers. This means is obviously incompatible with the system the Six have quite naturally set up for themselves.

The system of the Six consists of making a pool of the agricultural products of the entire community, of strictly determining their prices, of forbidding subsidizing, of organizing their consumption between all the members and of making it obligatory for each of these members to pay to the Community any savings they might make by having foodstuffs brought in from outside instead of consuming those offered by the Common Market.

Once again, what is to be done to make Britain, such as it is, enter that system?

One was sometimes led to believe that our English friends,

in applying for membership in the Common Market, agreed to change their own ways even to the point of applying all the conditions accepted and practiced by the Six, but, the question is to know if Great Britain can at present place itself, with the Continent and like it, within a tariff that is truly common, give up all preference with regard to the Commonwealth, cease to claim that its agriculture be privileged and, even more, consider as null and void the commitments it has made with the countries that are part of its free trade area. That question is the one at issue.

One cannot say that it has now been resolved. Will it be so one day? Obviously Britain alone can answer that.

The question is raised all the more since, following Britain, other States which are, I repeat, linked to it in the free trade area, for the same reasons as Great Britain, would or will want to enter the Common Market.

It must be agreed that the entry first of Great Britain and then that of those other States will completely change the series of adjustments, agreements, compensations and regulations already established between the Six, because all these States, like Britain, have very important traits of their own. We would then have to envisage the construction of another Common Market. But the 11-member, then 13-member and then perhaps 18-member Common Market that would be built would, without any doubt, hardly resemble the one the Six have built.

Moreover, this Community, growing in that way, would be confronted with all the problems of its economic relations with a crowd of other States, and first of all with the United States.

It is foreseeable that the cohesion of all its members, who would be very numerous and very diverse, would not hold for long and that in the end there would appear a colossal Atlantic Community under American dependence and leadership which would soon completely swallow up the European Community.

This is an assumption that can be perfectly justified in the eyes of some, but it is not at all what France wanted to do and what France is doing, which is a strictly European construction.

Then, it is possible that Britain would one day come round to transforming itself enough to belong to the European

Community without restriction and without reservation, and placing it ahead of anything else, and in that case the Six would open the door to it and France would place no obstacle in its path, although obviously the mere membership of Britain in the Community would completely change its nature and its volume.

It is also possible that England is not yet prepared to do this, and that indeed appears to be the outcome of the long, long Brussels talks. But if this is the case, there is nothing there that can be dramatic.

First of all, whatever decision Britain finally makes in this regard, there is no reason, as far as we are concerned, for the relations we have with it to be changed in any way. The consideration and the respect due that great State and that great people will not be altered in the least.

What Britain has done over the centuries and throughout the world is recognized as gigantic, even though there have often been conflicts with France. The glorious participation of Great Britain in the victory that crowned the First World War, we French will always admire. As for the role played by Britain at the most dramatic and decisive moment of the Second World War, no one has the right to forget it.

Truly, the fate of the free world, and first of all our own and even that of the United States and of Russia, has depended to a large extent on the resolution, the solidity and the courage of the British people such as Churchill gave them the will to be. This very day no one can dispute the fitness and the valour of the British.

Therefore, I repeat, if the Brussels negotiations were not to succeed at this time, nothing would prevent the conclusion of an agreement of association between the Common Market and Great Britain in such a way as to safeguard trade; neither would anything prevent the maintenance of the close relations between Britain and France and the continuation and development of their direct co-operation in all fields, especially those of science, technology and industry as, indeed, the two countries have just proven by deciding on the joint construction of the supersonic 'Concorde' aircraft.

Lastly, it is highly possible that Great Britain's own evolution and the evolution of the world would lead the British to the

Continent, whatever may be the delays before complete realization. For my part, this is what I am inclined to believe, and that is why, in my opinion, it will be in any case a great honour for the British Prime Minister, for my friend Harold Macmillan, and for his Government, to have perceived this so early, to have had enough political courage to proclaim it and to have had their country take the first steps along the path that, one day perhaps, will bring it to make fast to the Continent.

Question: What is France's position concerning the Kennedy multilateral formula, that is to say, concerning the Nassau agreements?

Answer: I have already had occasion several times to indicate publicly France's policy from the standpoint of its defence and also on the means with which, consequently, it deemed it necessary to equip itself. This time again I am going to try to clarify the subject. In any case I repeat after having said it often, that France intends to have its national defence. It is obvious that one country, especially one such as ours, cannot in the present day and age, and could not conduct a major modern war all by itself. To have allies goes without saying for us in the historic period we are in. But also for a great people to have the free disposition of itself and the means to struggle to preserve it is an absolute imperative, for alliances have no absolute virtues, whatever may be the sentiments on which they are based. And if one spontaneously loses, even for a while, the free disposition of oneself, there is a strong risk of never regaining it. And then, the conditions in which we presently find ourselves also make it imperative for us to act in this manner.

We are in the atomic age and we are a country that can be destroyed at any moment unless the aggressor is deterred from the undertaking by the certainty that he too will suffer frightful destruction. This justifies both alliance and independence. The Americans, our allies and our friends, have for a long time, alone, possessed a nuclear arsenal. So long as they alone had such an arsenal and so long as they showed their will to use it immediately if Europe were attacked—for at that time Europe alone could be attacked—the Americans acted in such a way that for France the question of an invasion hardly arose, since an attack was beyond all probability. It was then a matter for the Atlantic Alliance, that is to say, for the American command, of having in Europe and America a tactical and strategic air force capable of using atomic weapons—for at that time only airplanes could do that—and thus capable of protecting Europe. It was also a matter of lining up in Europe itself conventional land, naval and air forces which could ensure the deployment and use of atomic weapons. It can be said that, during that period, the deterrent worked and that there existed a practically insuperable obstacle to an invasion of Europe. It is impossible to overestimate the extent of the service, most fortunately passive, that the Americans at that time, in that way, rendered to the freedom of the world.

Since then, the Soviets have also acquired a nuclear arsenal, and that arsenal is powerful enough to endanger the very life of America. Naturally, I am not making an evaluation—if indeed it is possible to find a relation between the degree of one death and the degree of another—but the new and gigantic fact is there. From then on, the Americans found and are finding themselves confronted with the possibility of direct destruction. Thus the immediate defence, and one can say privileged defence of Europe, and the military participation of the Europeans, which were one basic factor of their strategy, moved by the force of circumstances into second place. We have just witnessed this during the Cuban affair.

The Americans, finding themselves exposed to a direct atomic attack from the Caribbean, acted in such a way as to rid themselves of that menace and, if it had been necessary, to crush it without its having occurred either to them or to anyone else that the game would necessarily be played in Europe and without recourse to the direct assistance of the Europeans. Moreover, the means which they immediately decided to employ in order to counter a direct attack, whether it came from Cuba only or was combined with another originating elsewhere, these means were automatically set aside for something other than the defence of Europe, even if Europe had been attacked in its turn.

And then, above and beyond everything, the deterrent is now a fact for the Russians as for the Americans, which means that in the case of a general atomic war, there would inevitably be frightful and perhaps fatal destruction in both countries. In these conditions, no one in the world—particularly no one in America—can say if, where, when, how and to what extent the American nuclear weapons would be employed to defend Europe. Moreover, this does not in the least prevent the American nuclear weapons, which are the most powerful of all, from remaining the essential guarantee of world peace. This fact, and the determination with which President Kennedy used it, came into full light out of the Cuban affair. But it remains that the American nuclear power does not necessarily and immediately meet all the eventualities concerning Europe and France.

Thus principles and realities combine to lead France to equip itself with an atomic force of its own. This does not at all exclude, of course, the combination of the action of this force with the action of the similar forces of its allies. But, for us, in this specific case, integration is something that is unimaginable. Indeed, as you know, we have begun with our own and only means to invent, test and construct atomic bombs and the vehicles for launching them.

It is completely understandable that this French undertaking does not appear to be highly satisfactory to certain American circles. In politics and in strategy, as in the economy, monopoly quite naturally appears to the person who holds it to be the best possible system. Then we hear a multiple choir of Americans—unofficial persons, experts and journalists—violently and strongly attacking our autonomous armament. 'The atomic force with which France intends to equip itself is and will remain,' they say, 'insignificant in relation to those of the United States and Russia. To build it up is thus to waste a lot of effort and money for nothing. And then, within the Alliance, the United States has an overwhelming superiority, therefore no one should run counter to its strategy through any divergent action.'

It is quite true that the number of nuclear weapons with which we can equip ourselves will not equal, far from it, the mass of those of the two giants of today. But since when has it been proved that a people should remain deprived of the most effective weapons for the reason that its chief possible adversary and its chief friend have means far superior to its own?

France, when formerly it was its turn to be a world colossus, often experienced the worth of either the resistance of a less powerful but well equipped adversary, or the support of an ally lining up inferior but well tempered and well employed weapons.

Moreover, the atomic force has a feature of its own, in that it has an efficacy that is certain and to an extent that is frightening even if it does not approach the conceivable maximum. In 1945 two bombs, then elementary, led Japan, who was not able to answer back, to capitulate. I do not want to evoke here the possibilities in which Europe could suffer nuclear actions that would be localized, but whose political and psychological consequences would be immense, unless there is a certainty that retaliation to that extent would be immediately unleashed. I only want to say that the French atomic force, from the very beginning of its establishment, will have the sombre and terrible capability of destroying in a few seconds millions and millions of men. This fact cannot fail to have at least some bearing on the intents of any possible aggressor.

Then, in the Bahamas, America and Britain concluded an agreement and we were asked to subscribe to it ourselves. Of course, I am only speaking of this proposal and agreement because they have been published and because their content is known. It is a question of constituting a so-called multilateral atomic force, in which Britain would turn over the weapons it has and will have and in which the Americans would place a few of their own. This multilateral force is assigned to the defence of Europe and is under the American NATO command. It is nevertheless understood that the British retain the possibility of withdrawing their atomic weapons for their own use should supreme national interest seem to them to demand it.

As for the bulk of American nuclear weapons, it remains outside the multilateral force and under the direct orders of the President of the United States. Furthermore, and in a way by compensation, Britain may purchase from America, if it so desires, Polaris missiles which are, as you know, launched from submarines specially built for that purpose and which carry the thermonuclear warheads adapted to them for a distance of 1,100–2,000 miles. To build these submarines and warheads, the British receive privileged assistance from the Americans. You know—I say this in passing—that this assistance was never offered to us and you should know, despite what some report, that we have never asked for it.

France has taken note of the Anglo-American Nassau agreement. As it was conceived, undoubtedly no one will be surprised that we cannot subscribe to it. It truly would not be useful for us to buy Polaris missiles when we have neither the submarines to launch them nor the thermonuclear warheads to arm them. Doubtless the day will come when we will have these submarines and these warheads. But that day will be long in coming. For the world war, the invasion and their consequences have slowed us down a great deal in our atomic development. When we will one day have these submarines and these warheads, what will the Polaris missiles then be worth? At that time we will probably have missiles of our own invention. In other words, for us, in terms of technology, this affair is not the question of the moment.

But also, it does not meet with the principle about which I just spoke and which consists of disposing in our own right of our deterrent force. To turn over our weapons to a multilateral force, under a foreign command, would be to act contrary to that principle of our defence and our policy. It is true that we too can theoretically retain the ability to take back in our hands, in the supreme hypothesis, our atomic weapons incorporated in the multilateral force. But how could we do it in practice during the unheard of moments of the atomic apocalypse? And then, this multilateral force necessarily entails a web of liaisons, transmissions and interferences within itself, and on the outside a ring of obligations such that, if an integral part were suddenly snatched from it, there would be a strong risk of paralysing it just at the moment, perhaps, when it should act.

In sum, we will adhere to the decision we have made: to construct and, if necessary, to employ our atomic force ourselves. And that without refusing, of course, co-operation, be it technological or strategic, if this co-operation is, on the other hand, desired by our allies.

Several questions were put to me on the subject of Germany.

These are of current interest since we shall be having the great honour and great pleasure of receiving the Chancellor and a number of his Ministers here in a few weeks' time.

Question: On the eve of your talks with the Chancellor, how do you envisage the evolution of Franco–German co-operation?

Answer: I hope that this question more or less covers all the others on the subject and to which I shall reply together.

Among the new elements that are in the process of shaping the world at present, I believe that there is none more striking and more fruitful than the Franco–German Pact. Two great peoples, which have for so long and so terribly opposed and fought each other, are now turning towards each other with the same impulse of sympathy and understanding. It is not only a question of a reconciliation demanded by circumstances. What is happening in reality is a kind of mutual discovery of two neighbours, each noticing the extent to which the other is valid, worthy and attractive.

It is from this then that springs the desire for a *rapprochement* manifest everywhere in the two countries which conforms with reality and which commands politics, because for the first time in many generations, the Germans and Gauls realize their solidarity. This solidarity exists obviously from the standpoint of their security, since the same threat of foreign domination confronts them and because their territories constitute a single strategic area. It exists from the economic standpoint because, for each of them, mutual trade is an essential and preponderant element. It exists from the standpoint of their cultural influence and development, for in thought, philosophy, science, the arts and technology they are complementary.

And now the voice of the peoples makes it heard that these currents deeply reflect something decisive and, without a doubt, something historic. Already, when President Luebke, in our capital, and later when Chancellor Adenauer, officially in Paris and in the Provinces, visited France, there arose from our people such homage and such testimony that there could be no doubt about the completely new course—to say the least—that feelings in our country had taken. When I myself, last September, had the honour of bearing the greetings of the French people to Germany, when I was received in Bonn,

Cologne, Düsseldorf, Duisburg, Hamburg, Munich, Stuttgart and other cities, all those who were able to see and hear were overwhelmed by the elemental and extraordinary outburst of enthusiasm displayed then in favour of the friendship of Germany and France, of the union of Europe as they both wish it and of their common action in the world. I for my part—I must admit—I was touched by it to the very depths of my soul and strengthened in my conviction that the new policy of Franco–German relations is based on an incomparable popular basis.

Now, all along this policy has been—we must pay him this tribute—that of Chancellor Adenauer. This great statesman has never ceased to think and to proclaim that Franco–German co-operation was an absolute necessity for the life and modern development of the two countries; that it was also the condition and the very basis of the construction of Europe; and finally that it was at present the most basic factor in the security of our continent and perhaps, in the future, a factor of balance and peace among the nations that people our continent from East to West. Since we think in exactly the same way, the Governments in Bonn and Paris did not have much difficulty in reaching an agreement to draw closer together in practice their relations in the political, economic, cultural and defence sectors.

The Franco–German meeting that will shortly be held here will permit us, we most sincerely hope, to organize our co-operation better than it is organized already. It goes without saying that there is nothing there that either resembles or tends towards the building up between Germany and France of some kind of exclusive community. The two countries have decided and are committed to being an integral part of Europe, such as it is built on the basis of the Rome Treaty. Moreover, it is absolutely impossible to see how the more effective *rapprochement* between the French and German peoples would in any way whatsoever harm the fraternity of Italy and France, a fraternity that is two thousand years old and which is today more alive than ever, or harm the close links that the centuries have forged between us and Belgium, the Netherlands and Luxembourg.

But it is true that by tightening their co-operation, Germany and France are setting an example which may be useful to the co-operation of everyone.

Question: I had asked you if the army of the German Federal Republic, deployed where it is and commanded as it is, could be equipped with and dispose of nuclear arms?

Answer: Sir, in this case it is up to Federal Germany to say what it wishes and to conduct its own policy. You have seen that in the matter of defence France conducts its own. It is evident that there is close solidarity between the defence of Germany and that of France, but each country is master in its own house and I shall not answer for the German Government.

Question: Since you have stated many times, in your previous speeches, that when the time came France would say what contribution she intended to make towards disarmament, do you not believe that the time has come to discuss this?

Answer: I do not see how disarmament is being enforced. Periodically the question arises between the United States and Soviet Russia, both of which have enormous nuclear arsenals, of suspending their tests. That happens generally when they have both just completed a big series.

We have no objection to these two great States suspending their nuclear tests; but the fact that they might suspend them would in no way change their arsenals such as they are and would in no way be a disarmament measure. We have very frequently said that so long as forces exist in the world as they do, nothing can prevent France from acquiring one itself; but that if the day came when those arms would be really destroyed, France would wholeheartedly give up making them on its own account.

DOCUMENT 24. EXTRACTS FROM MR. HAROLD WILSON'S STRAS-BOURG SPEECH 23 JANUARY 1967

We who are citizens of this great continent have the right to take pride in the part we have played in history, not least in the creation of great—and themselves diverse—nations beyond the seas. And if in a rapidly shrinking world a great challenge we now face is that of coming to terms with the thrusting urgency of new populous, hungry nations, on a basis no longer so much of what we can take from them as of what we can give to them, there is nothing inward looking nor complacent in drawing on the richness of our own past here in Europe. And we can put forth, in all the massive strength of which we are capable, the effort we should make, and must make, on behalf of the new nations in Asia and Africa and Latin America—an effort that will call for really massive strength—if our Europe itself is united and strong.

Nor, again, can those nations here represented, with all the unexampled contribution we have it in our power to make to the achievement of peace, make that contribution unless we can achieve a greater unity of purpose. A unity of purpose which must be directed not only to the solution of our own problems in Europe—that wider Europe whose true boundaries transcend the man-made divisions deepened by two world wars—but which must be directed equally to the solution of the wider world problems which year by year constitute the pattern of international discussion at the United Nations . . .

This effort can never achieve its full purpose, whether in terms of development or of peace, unless we learn the way to build up, through a more real unity, our common economy and our mutual political strength.

For economic strength and political unity must develop together. And, just as we are all dedicated to the proposition that economic strength should be developed in an outward-looking sense, so every one of us is resolved that the political objective is not only to end the series of conflicts which have torn Europe apart twice in this century but to create first a dialogue and then a real and living peace with our neighbours to the east, and, still more widely, to strengthen the voice of each one of us in the councils of the world . . .

Ten weeks ago I announced in Parliament . . . that the Government had decided that a new high-level approach must now be made to see whether the conditions existed—or did not exist—for fruitful negotiations, and the basis on which such negotiations could take place. And I said to the House of Commons:

'I want the House, the country, and our friends abroad to

know that the Government are approaching the discussions I have foreshadowed with the clear intention and determination to enter the European Economic Community if, as we hope, our essential British and Commonwealth interests can be safeguarded. We mean business.'

That, Mr. President, is our position. We mean business. And I am going to say why we mean business.

We mean business because we believe that British entry and the involvement of other EFTA countries, whether by entry or association, will of themselves contribute massively to the economic unity and strength of Europe. What is today a market of about 180 millions becomes a potential market of nearly 280 millions, the biggest among all the industrially advanced countries, west or east.

Not only consumers, but producers, too. The adherence of most or all of the EFTA countries would bring to the existing communities not only a wider market but also the skill, the expertise, the science and technology of millions of workers and thousands upon thousands trained in the highest refinements of modern technology.

We mean business again because the interests of Europe as a whole—wider Europe no less than those of western, northern and southern Europe—will be served, as equally our own separate interests will be served, by creating a greater and more powerful economic community. I have always made clear that, in my view, the concept of a powerful Atlantic partnership can be realized only when Europe is able to put forth her full economic strength so that we can in industrial affairs speak from strength to our Atlantic partners.

Let no one here doubt Britain's loyalty to NATO and the Atlantic Alliance. But I have also always said that that loyalty must never mean subservience. Still less must it mean an industrial helotry under which we in Europe produce only the conventional apparatus of a modern economy while becoming increasingly dependent on American business for the sophisticated apparatus which will call the industrial tune in the 70s and 80s.

We mean business in a political sense because over the next year, the next ten years, the next twenty years, the unity of

Europe is going to be forged, and geography, history, interest and sentiment alike demand that we play our part in forging it—and working it.

There may be those who believe that to widen the community will be to weaken it or to dilute its existing sense of purpose and its institutions. Change there will be, as there has been throughout these ten years. For he who rejects change is the architect of decay. The only human institution which rejects progress is the cemetery. We within Europe will play our full part in generating change, whatever that means for vested interests or for the protectionist-minded, in Britain or elsewhere. It will be not on stagnation but on movement, continual movement, that the momentum created in postwar Europe can continue, indeed accelerate. Widening therefore, based on change, will mean not weakening, but strengthening.

I have said that Britain will gain if the right conditions can be established for a decisive and urgent move forward. But equally let no one here underestimate what Britain can also contribute.

We shall be bringing, not only to the council chamber but to the power house of Europe, a new, more determined Britain, a Britain whose answer to the sick jibes of some commentators is being given not in words but in deeds . . .

Besides an economy growing in strength we bring all that British technology has to offer. Let us not be defeatist about Europe's technological contribution compared with that of the United States. Each European country can speak for itself. But what would the American industrial economy look like today without jet aircraft, directly based on a British invention freely made available as part of our war effort; antibiotics— similarly made over; the electronic revolution based on the British development of radar; indeed, the entire nuclear superstructure which could never have been created except on the basic research of Rutherford and other British scientists. If this is our decision, I hope the negotiations will be on a minimum number of broad issues and not on an infinity of details.

Many of the details, many of the consequential decisions— important though they be—can best be settled on a continuing basis from within the Community . . .

197

But I should be less than frank if I did not at least refer to the problems created particularly by the financial aspects of the Community's agricultural policy, by arrangements made and appropriately, to secure fairness and equity between the agricultural interests of the six countries concerned; but arrangements which do not reflect—clearly they could not reflect—the problem created by the entry of a major food-importing nation such as Britain.

For they would mean a financial contribution which would fundamentally affect not only the balance so painfully worked out two years ago but also the balance of equity, as well as the balance of payments, between Britain—and other countries who would seek to join—and the existing Six.

To outline this question, and to be aware of others, is not designed to evoke any spirit of depression, still less defeatism. These problems are there to be overcome. I believe they can be overcome, given the same spirit of constructive ingenuity, tolerance and understanding, give and take, which have animated the relations of the six members in their dealings with one another from the outset . . .

In the last century the creation of the nation states of Europe called on the citizens of those nations to sacrifice their lives. In this century the future of Europe, and of the world, has twice required a generation of men to give their lives in the defence of freedom. The Europe of today, the Europe it is in our power to fashion, with all that this means for a wider world, calls for no such heroic sacrifices—the sacrifices which are asked of this generation are sacrifices only of supposed short-term interests, of short-term prejudices and stereotyped modes of thought. I believe that this generation has decided on its answer.

CONCLUSION

I

The historical introduction to this book sought to tell the story of how the European Economic Community came into being, the methods by which it is now setting up a European Common Market, and the tentative groping over the past twenty years for a European Community that transcends the economic sphere. The emergence of something which, as a pattern, has not yet crystallized can be told only in teleological terms: only by seeing events through the eyes of those who have a Community model in mind can we find any coherent story to tell. (A book on Germany could treat the defeat of EDC as a positive step in the process by which West Germany attained national sovereignty; a historian of France could treat it as part of the overall pattern of politics in the Fourth Republic; but a book on the European Community cannot but treat it as a negative event, as a break in the emergent total pattern on which the very title of the book demands we should focus.) And similarly—while the opponents of the pattern have of course been allowed a look in too—many of the documents have illustrated ideas that have not yet come to fruition: the very subject of the book remains for the moment less of a reality than an aspiration.

The documents of course have been chosen to convey some of the peculiar local 'feel' and colour of this particular, intensely European venture, to show up the terminology and imagery of its champions and its opponents, and to display distinctions between the various schools of thought as to the direction in which the European idea should be developed— whether according to a Gaullist concept, towards European federalism, or towards an Atlantic Community. These final pages, by contrast, will try to consider this particular experiment in Western Europe in more general theoretical terms, less as a specific historical and geographical event than as a paradigm or 'model' for the exploration of some of the problems facing modern international relations.

Now in model-building the economist (and the student of other aspects of society too) tries neither to describe the present nor to predict the future or to prescribe an optimum: he merely abstracts certain strategic variables from the intractable mass of sheer data, much as a scientist artificially isolates elements not normally found in a pure state in nature, in order to examine their interactions and implications. Similarly this concluding personal assessment concentrates on only one or two among a number of recent trends to focus discussion on such problems as they are already raising and may come to pose increasingly in the future. Whether these trends really form the mainstream of present historical development or not, in this brief discussion we shall have to neglect both the back-wash and the back-waters—even if at times, it must be admitted, these seem to be only too obvious and even on other interpretations appear dominant.

II

Within the life-time of the last generation, the curve of man's technical progress (almost regardless of what criterion we use, the number of people one man can address or kill at one time, the weight he can shift, the speed of his movement, the distance from land he can venture and so forth), after millennia of horizontal progression and a few centuries of only very slight upward trend, has suddenly curled into an all but vertical direction. Our inbuilt inductive mechanism, our instinctive expectation that the future will resemble the past (which has immense survival value for us as for other living species in a constant natural environment) thus becomes a source of immense danger: for whatever the future may be like, we now know that it will be nothing like the past and that the only constant factor today (if any) is the rate of acceleration in the speed of change. We can therefore no longer approach the social problems of the future with the ingrained habits and modes of thinking of earlier centuries—whether the Old Testament or Machiavelli, *The Wealth of Nations* or *Das Kapital:* the old codices cannot solve problems that can be apprehended in their full complexity only by the new computers.

If we try to make explicit the fundamental presuppositions in our picture of society, most of us I suspect really take for granted the basic eighteenth-century model of *cuius regio eius religio*. First, that the surface of the globe is split (or even falls naturally) into mutually exclusive *regios*, little geographical compartments over each of which there is a *rex*, a single political authority with unlimited power (or at least the power to determine its own power) over that limited spatial area. Secondly, this principle implied that inside each of these regions there was (or should be) a single *religio*, a dominant philosophy of life, to transgress against which would be 'un-American', *undeutsch*, or 'not cricket'.

Over the past fifteen or even twenty years, however, the dangers of the new technology, the pressures of the rising density of the earth's human population, but above all the terrific complexity of our new problems, which none of our traditional ideologists could possibly have foreseen, have forced on us a new tolerance and a new empiricism, and will I believe force us to go much further still in that direction in the future. Over the past fifteen years we have seen the decline of McCarthyism in the United States, of Stalinism in the Soviet Union, and of traditional clericalism in the Catholic Church; and capitalism and socialism, in the new pragmatic atmosphere, no longer stand like cliffs over against each other either intellectually or in the practical running of modern industrial societies. Such a concentration, now forced on us, on the actual data of practical problems to be solved rather than on the ideological approaches into which their solutions might be fitted, should—as it has already begun to do, since the Cuban confrontation and indeed earlier—allow far more co-operation, even collusion, between what used to be called the blocs in the joint solution of common practical problems.

But even more striking in a way has been a second trend— that away from the concept of the *regio* and the *rex*—not, certainly, in Africa and Asia and other countries called 'developing' because they are not developing anything like fast enough—but in the maturer industrial parts of the world. There the increasing demands of scale and the increasing international interdependence of modern economics, communications and defence requirements have made many of the regional sub-divisions impractical if not impracticable in respect of a wide variety of functions of government. It may be that cheaper de Gaulle-type do-it-yourself atom bombs and tactical nuclear weapons may in defence give a certain respite to the nation state of the 50 million size; but broadly speaking the continuing acceleration in the rate of technical change is likely to make the opportunity cost of purely national organization even greater in the future.

As a consequence we have seen attempts, which we might for heuristic purposes classify as being mainly of two types, to supplement or even replace the nation state: both types have been advocated, if not actually seriously attempted, both on the regional and on the ecumenical (or near-ecumenical) scale, both have been advocated as 'closed' or as essentially 'open' organizations. (It is worth noting that EEC is doubly a 'closed' organization, being open only to European states and only to those unanimously admitted by the existing members.) Let us call the two types constitutional or federal, and co-operative or intergovernmental kinds of organization.

Thus we have on the one hand had ideals such as those of world government or of a United States of Europe seeking to by-pass the component nation state and base a new supra-sovereignty on a new constitutional document issued ultimately in the name of 'We, the People'—ideals that have in effect put the cart before the horse in their once-and-for-all radicalism and remain unrealized both on the European and on the world scale. On the other hand there is the more modest approach, which argues that it is only very limited specific functions that require organization on a scale wider than that of the traditional national unit, and believes that these can be co-ordinated by purely functional intergovernmental co-operation which need at no point detract from the legal sovereignty of any Member State. This has scored concrete successes up to a point. GATT, the IMF, and the EPU are examples of multilateral arrangements which—without too directly raising ideological and constitutional problems and without detracting from legal freedom of action—can, by sanctions and rewards, substantially modify it (usually by reducing the effective range of choice open to each participant).

Between these two approaches there is a difference, rather

than a distinction, in the sense that these in practice if not in law are points on a scale: for the sanctions and rewards are absolutely automatic only in a highly detailed international treaty, with an element of uncertitude and discretion more usually left open for negotiation between the partners in the light of circumstances arising, so that the need for mutual accommodation of standpoints, while not eliminating a formal veto, in practice places limits on its use and a premium on albeit reluctant agreement.

Nevertheless the Community method as exemplified in EEC is not simply a compromise form between the two but a third, different in kind from both the types of organization just sketched: for both are instantaneous, or static, arrangements in law, even if in practice the passage of time may make them more (or alternatively less) restrictive on national freedom of action. The Community treaties are the only ones (at least known to me) which have built into them a systematic time-dimension, which are progressive not only as to the substance but far more important as to the procedure: which progressively limit national veto powers partly with the automatic passage of time, partly by default of a national veto on the original time-table (so far as the passage from the first to the second stage was concerned). They are thus not a point situated somewhere on the scale of intergovernmental to federal organization, but constitute an institutionalized movement along it: if you like not a rung somewhere on the ladder, but in effect an escalator from intergovernmental to constitutional organization.

III

The 'Europeans' recognized the reality of the nation-state and did not believe that common institutions, set up in a vacuum, could somehow create a common interest: they believed that common institutions must be developed concurrently with common interests and must interact with them, intensify them and thereby make further common institutions both necessary and practicable. So they used a pragmatic technique, exploiting particular tactical situations in order to set up new institutions, which helped solve other problems but also in their turn themselves raised new problems that could be resolved only by further snowball progress along this same road.

This movement of European integration has in fact taken the form of a dialectic, of thesis and antithesis that can be reconciled only by a new imaginative step forward into a higher level of integration each time. It started from the bottom upwards with the problem of the Ruhr. The Allies were determined that Germany must never regain control of her coal and steel resources: but one could not discriminate against any one country for ever. To this antithesis there was only one synthesis: that other nations should abdicate the same measure of control over their coal and steel resources that they intended the Germans never to regain. This precisely was the achievement of the Schuman Plan.

The institution of the Coal and Steel Community really had two main effects. The only territorial dispute between France and Germany at the conclusion of the Second World War was over the Saar—a territory that chiefly matters because of the coal and steel it produces. Once coal and steel were pooled anyway between France, Germany, and other Community partners, this bitter dispute suddenly became not so much solved as dissolved: the shift in the whole context of Franco-German relations made the quarrel over coal and steel meaningless, and so the path lay open for further agreement between these two historic enemies.

The other effect of the Coal and Steel Community consisted not in the problems the Community solved, but in the new problems it raised—consisted in fact in the planned anomaly of this partial economic integration itself. How could there be a common policy for coal when there was none for oil or for natural gas or for atomic energy, when there was no harmonization of transport or labour policy? And if transport rates and labour policy are harmonized for coal and for steel, how can the rest of transport and labour policy continue to diverge? Again it was progress by a dialectical process; and from integration in two sectors of the economy the Six went forward to their general Economic Community.

At this point one must look for a moment at the institutional technique of this Community method of integration. It has, I think, three features remarkable above all.

First, each Treaty setting up one of the three existing Com-

munities contains a rigid backbone of precise commitments—
in the case of EEC a detailed twelve-year plan agreed on in
advance, signed, sealed, and delivered come what may. Just as
on the level of successive Community constructions there was
an implicit strategy of long-term integration, an attempt to
trigger off a dynamic that would gather its own momentum, so
at the level of the institutional tactics the precise obligations
were meant to set rolling a snowball movement. On the one
side they were to force the pace for further mutual commitments
as time goes on and step up the need to agree on joint policies.
On the other hand they were also to facilitate such further
agreements through the sheer passage of time, through con-
solidating mutual confidence between the countries working
together within the Community, and through increasing the
congruence of their substantial interests.

The Six have in fact on almost every matter gone faster along
this precisely predetermined course than the Treaty itself
demands. But then it must be remembered also that these
are all the easier matters and on the whole the negative ones,
outstandingly of course the mutual abolition of industrial
tariffs. The more difficult things and the positive things—the
joint planning in a host of different fields, the real meat of
integration to which the freeing of trade is but a preliminary
—could not be laid down in treaty form ten or twelve years
ahead of execution In fact if the Six had decided to debate all
the problems that might be encountered in circumstances as
yet unforeseen in 1956 (in the way attempted in the negotiations for British entry in 1961–3), the drafting of the Rome
Treaty would still be going on today, or, more likely, would
have been abandoned long ago.

Joined on to the rigid backbone of precise commitments
there are therefore what I would like to call the muscles:
agreements, not on matters of substance, but simply
agreements-to-agree on common policies hereafter by certain
procedures and by certain deadlines: setting up in fact certain
political institutions to take economic decisions by methods
transcending the national veto.

For, thirdly, the Treaty sets up Community institutions
independent of the member governments. It is these institutions
that propose the policies, it is they that act, if one may continue

the metaphor, as the brain that directs the muscles within the limits set by the skeleton Treaty. Such Community policies can and must be framed, not to reconcile the different national policies that are designed to solve partial problems or even to deflect them on to the next country, but to deal with the problem itself as it presents itself at Community level and to deal with it from a Community point of view, in the interests of all the Community's citizens regardless of nationality.

The Commission, representing the distinct interest of 180 million inhabitants rather than the partial interests of separate national populations, is injected into the decision-making mechanism almost as a seventh player, with its own weight and of course also with a vested interest of its own.

But the final decision on the major policies are taken not by the Commission of the Community itself, but by the national governments in the Council of Ministers. At the beginning, any one Government could veto the Commission's proposals; but as time goes on the Treaty lays down that votes on a vast range of subjects need not be taken unanimously any more: a qualified majority is sufficient, so that it takes at least two governments to veto a proposal, not counting Luxembourg, and even all three Benelux states can be overruled. Here again this is not a federal structure but a Community system *sui generis*, in which the Community organs propose but the national governments dispose according to voting rules drawn up with a time dimension, rules that progressively limit the veto power of any one state alone.

The supranational Commission and its role of initiative in the common interest, the interpenetration of national and Community civil services, the 'infranational' Community organization of parties and pressure-groups, and the sheer intensity of contact, machinery, convergence of interest, and political will and leadership make it very difficult to tell just which eggs have contributed to which part of the omelette— indeed this may well be a chemical rather than a purely aggregative process.

Now, of course, institutions are not enough: they are no substitute for policies, or for their execution. It is the policies and their execution that matter. But without the institutions, as we have seen all too often, the right policies are difficult enough to formulate and all too often quite impossible to adopt and then to execute. And what is more, there is a profound inner link between political forms and their content, between institutional structures and the external policies they are designed to pursue. This really is what makes nonsense of the question so often put in the past whether the Common Market was primarily an economic or a political enterprise, almost as if there were two sorts of questions political and economic, as there are two sorts of animals—elephants and giraffes. That I think is what some logicians call a 'type fallacy', an assumption that political questions and economic questions, and even the words 'political' and 'economic', are of the same type. But when we look at politics today, politics, even in the national context, are about a whole variety of different things. About morality laws, about nuclear strategy, about educational policy, about foreign policy, and so forth: but probably the biggest group of subjects that we debate in our national politics today is that of economic subjects. Politics in fact is not the name of a subject, as it were yet another animal, but politics is the name of the arena in which these different animals appear. A question is political not because of what it is about, the word 'political' tells us something not about the subject that is being dealt with, but about the manner in which it is being treated. Whenever as a community we decide to argue a question through to a common decision, that question becomes political: and so the Economic Community because it transfers to Brussels a range of decisions which have hitherto been taken within the context of national politics, because it deals with problems that are of immense direct impact on the lives of the voters, on the peasants and on the miners, on the consumers and on the industrial workers of these countries, the Economic Community is political precisely because it is economic. And that is why from the antithesis between centralized decisions taken on a Community basis and on a Community scale on the one hand, and the need for democratic control of decision-making, of policy-making on the other, those who built the new European Communities always felt—and they always said so in the preambles to their treaties and in all their speeches—that an Economic Community must lead to a Political Community in which in the last resort a European Parliament would be directly elected and a European executive would be directly responsible to it. And then, they hoped, from this increasing intensity of joint political decision-making in the economic domain there might follow also a spill-over into other fields of joint decision-taking—notably in the spheres of foreign policy and even defence.

IV

Over the past three years since the French veto on Britain's accession to the EEC the thesis of a dialectic of intensity has of course been subjected to severe tests. We could distinguish three periods in the Community's political history—the early relatively amicable honeymoon until January 1963, when President de Gaulle in effect vetoed Britain's entry into EEC; the next two and a half years, when it looked as if a fundamental cleavage of foreign and defence policy did not prove to be any insuperable obstacle to economic integration; and the seven months' crisis of July 1965 to January 1966. This last really went to show that the process of economic integration had gone so far, the costs of pulling out had risen so high, and the other Five were now so prepared to stand together to face French intransigence and insist on the integrity of the Treaty, that President de Gaulle's bluff was in effect called, and economic integration would continue not only in spite of differences of foreign and defence policy, but also in spite of conflicting views of the political mechanisms governing economic integration itself.

The notion of a 'political take-off'—a point beyond which it really becomes easier to let the integration process continue or even to accelerate it than to brake or halt it—seems to emerge from the tougher test of the last three years uncontroverted. Even at the height of the crisis in 1965 President de Gaulle's whole stance was the defensive one of a man trying to arrest or roll back a process that had gathered if not strictly speaking autonomous momentum then at least a momentum that seriously handicapped its opponents, and made progress correspondingly easier for those with the political will to press on.

Of course it can be argued that the whole machine has been creaking dangerously ever since it started work, that the Community has in fact ever since 1961 been lurching from crisis to crisis. In December 1961 they stopped the clock and continued negotiations until (after two heart attacks and one nervous collapse among the participants) they reached agreement at 5 a.m. on Sunday morning 14 January to pass on from the first to the second stage of the transition period. A year later, President de Gaulle stopped our negotiations with the Six which had gone from 'crunch' to 'crunch' by his press conference on 14 January 1963, in effect vetoing British entry and thus triggered off another crisis between the Community's members. At the end of 1964 they were again tensely negotiating against the clock on agricultural policy. In mid-1965 there was yet another bitter negotiation against a deadline, this time mainly on the financing of the farm fund, and when midnight on 30 June came without agreement, the French chairman closed the negotiations and France was absent from every intergovernmental meeting of the Community until she came back in January 1966.

Each time the commentators announced that this was the gravest crisis the Common Market had yet faced. Each time they were probably right. Each time there were prophets of immediate disintegration. Each time so far they were wrong. Certainly the last and most protracted crisis of them all has for the first time involved the withdrawal of a country from the institutions of the Community, and President de Gaulle's press conference of 10 September constituted the most radical attack on the whole constitutional system of the Community made by any head of a member state so far. When it was resolved, there were again commentators (as there were after most of the other crises) to say that the Common Market had now passed the point of no return—yet another point of no return, some would say—and in a sense (or at least in that lesser sense) they too were right. Each crisis surmounted has not only taken economic integration a step further, but also—so far at least—has strengthened the cohesion of the Six and increased their skill and determination to surmount future crises. In a sense perhaps the newspapers (for the usual sets of reasons) have taken each successive crisis rather too seriously. But at the same time I suspect they have taken the recurring phenomenon of crisis as a political institution nothing like seriously enough.

Among the many constitutional and semantic differences

that hamper communication across the Channel, the notion of 'crisis' holds an honourable place. French and Italian politics have had long periods in which the governmental process consisted of alternations between crises and the resulting compromise policies of coalition governments—phenomena intimately related to the multi-party systems of these countries and perhaps difficult to conceive by those who regard a two-party system, or even the traditional bilateralism of industrial negotiations, as the norm for the process of reaching agreement. In French and Italian it is in fact hardly paradoxical to call the crisis a constitutional mechanism of the Community and to say that its progress is, and moreover is designed to be, from one crisis and indeed *by* one crisis to the next.

The Community system, as we have seen, depends for its progress on multilateral negotiations over joint positive policies, and such negotiations in turn depend on almost artificially created crises for their success. There is no making of omelettes without the breaking of eggs. No one likes to see his own eggs go into the pan without others throwing theirs in too, and eggs are in this cuisine of very disparate values and sizes. Hence the function of the deadline, reflecting and intensifying the pressure of circumstances, when to their own chorus of 'ready, steady, go' the participants agree to make mutual sacrifices for the common good. No wonder that there are pitched arguments as to how many sacrifices each should make, which they should be, and what sort of offsetting concessions will have to be included in the next orgy of policy decisions at the next self-imposed deadline to balance the inequalities inherent in every package deal of such a complicated kind. It would be foolish to expect revolutions to progress smoothly and so far in fact one can only be surprised at the tameness with which six national political systems have accepted the threatened demolition of their sovereignty within the economic domain. On the other hand they have of course—with France setting the example—resisted any spill-over from the economic field to such others as foreign policy and defence.

V

These are questions of immediate relevance to the European Community. But in this concluding assessment we must pose the problem in rather more general terms. And once it is the process and not the area, the function and not the region, the method and not the substance we focus on, the question arises how independent the one is from the other. Can the Community technique be used for subjects other than economics or indeed must it be used, once you start, for *all* questions because all are connected? And how applicable, how adaptable, is the Community technique to groupings other than these particular Six?

Science advances by the death of beautiful hypotheses. Perhaps so far there is not enough evidence—not enough time has yet elapsed—to kill any of the different notions put forward about the process of European integration. In spite of very testing difficulties, nothing has yet falsified the notion of a 'dialectic of intensity' within the sphere of economic policy-making, and one could argue that there was some evidence accumulating in its favour. On the other hand there is little evidence so far for any 'spill-over effect' from economic integration into integration of policy in other domains, notably foreign policy and defence. On the contrary as we have seen in the short run real clashes of aim in these realms have been compatible with intensified economic integration.

There is a theoretical no less than a political problem here, not unrelated to the early disputes between functionalist and federalist theoreticians. Theorists of the nation state of course can base themselves on the indivisibility of sovereignty not simply in law, but in practical terms: all subjects interlock, and therefore no functions of the sovereign can be split off from his omnicompetence and his total responsibility and transferred to another authority; at most they can be temporarily and conditionally delegated to subordinate agencies. This is where the British Government's 'functionalism' of the nineteen-forties and President de Gaulle's present attitude come very close to each other. On the other hand federalists believe that a final static division can be made (whether within a national or a European federal system) between problems and therefore between the responsibility for solving or at least dealing with them; and the theoretical international functionalists would take the same line, even if they would leave residuary power in the component nation states and perhaps regard a supreme international political authority as secondary to the functional organizations.

The Community method in this sense is neither federal nor functional in its doctrine: it contemplates no final irrevocable static division of functions between different institutions. Whether or not all questions are ultimately linked is a metaphysical or a semantic issue. It is more realistic to recognize that questions are to some extent and for some time and to some degree separable from each other and the interesting fact surely is that different questions between different countries, and different countries over different questions, are linked in different ways with different degrees of technical intricacy, with different degrees of political urgency and with different degrees of temporal immediacy. The secret of the Community method then is to spot such concatenations of questions as yield a high ratio of welfare output to co-operative input, question tackling which forces the pace at the same time as it attenuates obstacles to further integration, all without running into linked problems of so difficult a kind that they stop the process altogether. It is rather like trying to pick up a completed jigsaw puzzle from the table—or at least trying to spot those pieces which will through their interlocking with others allow one with two fingers to pick up the largest amount of pieces without their getting so heavy that the whole thing drops to the ground. And I shall want to argue, finally, that this technique of weaving back and forth between different kinds of problem may be used even between different combinations of countries in order to advance the overall goal of fitting the industrialized world to deal not only with the East–West but also with the North–South problem of world development.

VI

In the heyday of 1962, when the EFTA countries were negotiating to join or become Associates of the EEC, and the United States under President Kennedy's doctrine of interdependence was passing the Trade Expansion Act as its reply to the potential challenge of an enlarged Community, it was possible to speak not only of a 'dialectic of intensity', but also of a 'dialectic of extension', by which the Community technique or at least the Community-type approach would have to be used outside the EEC to cope with the problems that the EEC's existence and policies posed to different sections of the outside world.

Even in 1956 the Six could not plan their new Community without taking into consideration what would happen as a result of the Common Market to the African and other countries which were then their colonies and now remain their associates. A few years later, before the common external tariff was even half way to being formed, there was a radical change of orientation in British foreign policy—what Hugh Gaitskell called 'a reversal of 1,000 years of British history' (some of the historians would probably say 400 years of British history but let's not quarrel about that). And then, just as if one passed an electric current through a scattering of iron filings which are pointing, some towards the Commonwealth, others across the Atlantic or towards Scandinavia and the rest—these all suddenly turned towards Brussels. So there was the reorientation of EFTA policy. All the Commonwealth countries suddenly had to take account of this new factor, and even now Nigeria has completed, and East Africa is beginning, negotiations for association with the Common Market despite the fact that Britain herself does not look like joining in the immediate future. And what is more, this reorientation towards this new magnetic centre by Britain, by Africa, by EFTA, by the Commonwealth also provoked the American response of the Trade Expansion Act and the attempt at the Kennedy Round.

The Brussels negotiations began as an attempt to fit Britain into the European Community, but thanks to Britain's overseas connections it very quickly turned into a consideration of how to fit the European Community into the structure of the world economy. In discussing Commonwealth food exports, the import of Asian manufactures and the position of sterling, Britain and the Community had their noses rubbed in far more general, but very serious problems: dilemmas which, though they may present themselves in bilateral guise, can be dissolved only if they are treated in global terms; difficulties which, though they may pose today in static terms, are capable of solution only if they are extrapolated into a rapidly evolving dynamic world framework.

Britain demanded special conditions for the Commonwealth

which would have resulted in preferential arrangements with Commonwealth countries. Now—except for their own ex-colonies, whose population is only one-twelfth of that of the Commonwealth—the Six had early on determined that they would abide by the non-discriminatory world trade code of the General Agreement on Tariffs and Trade, by which Britain, too, regards herself as bound. From this antithesis between intra-Commonwealth preferential arrangements and extra-Community non-discrimination, again, there could be only one logical way out: to submerge Britain's preferential demands for trade and commodity guarantees into world-wide solutions to world-wide trade and commodity problems.

President de Gaulle's veto and President Kennedy's death, the whole change in the Atlantic climate since then—in spite of the slight auguries for better things raised consequently at the Geneva Conference for Trade and Development—make that thesis appear perhaps premature as analysis, even if valid as an aspiration or advocacy for action. But more general questions remain. K. C. Wheare listed various pre-conditions as being to some extent prerequisites of federal government: not only the desire to be united for some but distinct for other purposes, but also the need for common defence, a desire to be independent of foreign powers, a hope of economic advantage, geographical neighbourhood, some prior political association and similarity of political institution. Must all these conditions be fulfilled to the hilt (even assuming Wheare to be right) whenever functional co-operation is to go beyond the purely intergovernmental? What sociological conditions, in particular, have to obtain for there to be hope of Community type arrangements to be instituted?

This question must be posed in relation to three types of area: areas outside the existing Community, wishing to integrate certain functions—most obvious of course are the Central American Common Market, LAFTA, the Arab Common Market Treaty—and, as a negative instance as it were, the East African Common Market; secondly, areas—most notably of course that now (by somewhat dubious geography) termed the North Atlantic, including the existing European Community (or overlapping it if one regards France's membership of NATO as gradually approaching the nugatory); and thirdly, the open or near-open ecumenical or near ecumenical extension, the area of the world.

The first of these three type questions may not yet affect us very immediately in Europe, but the second and third do concern Europe herself, the growing together of the regional European with the Atlantic institutions, and the regional role of the European and the Atlantic institutions in the web of world organization. For the Europeans therefore the questions are (a) how extensive can the existing intensive Community-type organizations become; (b) is there any case for new organizations intermediate in extension and intensity between the tight Community and the loose United Nations structures; and (c) how far can the existing specialized agencies of the United Nations be reinforced by the attrition or elimination of national vetoes?

The sphere of defence is one in which in NATO we have gone well beyond the intergovernmental approach already and if the Multilateral Force were ever to become a politically convincing concept we would have to go a great deal further along that road (at least the United States would have to accept the possibility of being outvoted). In GATT the 'chicken war' was resolved by a technique closely resembling in practice if not in law the supranational authority of a Community type. And if we have gone beyond the intergovernmental technique here no less than in different peace-keeping missions of the United Nations, what pre-conditions have to be fulfilled for progressive changes in institutions along this scale to be themselves institutionalized in advance?

I have tried to argue elsewhere that a reform of the International Monetary Fund, an effective Kennedy round, global solutions to the problems of temperate agriculture, and tropical commodity stabilization plans of the kind now canvassed at UNCTAD might materially require advances along these lines. But how can we fulfil the political pre-conditions they in turn require?

VII

Whether this model is taken as a caricature of existing states of affairs, a prophecy of inevitable brave new worlds, or as a messianic panacea, it leads—as self-respecting models should do—to a general theory: a two-dimensional organization of the world in which specific public functions hitherto exercised on a 'vertical' territorial basis are separated out and subtracted from traditional state sovereignty and—like many economic functions in EEC—reorganized 'horizontally' and joined up on a functional basis: in which the traditional single authority with unlimited power over a limited geographical area is partly replaced by a single authority with specifically limited powers over ultimately perhaps an unlimited geographical area.

There is no space here to elaborate such notions in detail, and in a sense it would be self-contradictory when advocating a Community approach also to define the exact stages to be gone through or the precise shape of the final solution— indeed perhaps even to believe that there could ever be anything like a 'final solution'. The whole point of the Community approach is its flexible step-by-step character, and as Dag Hammarskjöld once said: 'Working at the edge of the development of human society is to work on the brink of the unknown.' But what is clear is that the functional attack on all these problems—just like the Economic Community in Europe— will have political implications, this time on a far wider scale. Commodity arrangements and world development plans will require institutions to group together the interested industrial and developing countries on a basis of equality: and the more such important problems are dealt with by Community-type institutions, the more urgent will democratic supervision become. The existing Community institutions with their links to associated Africa, the Commonwealth consultative machinery, and other existing regional bodies could thus be reconstituted along Community lines, and could form, with revamped organs of the United Nations, a network of overlapping circles, untidy perhaps, but with an untidiness that reflects the functional character of each body, tailored in composition and structure precisely to fulfil a particular concrete task. In the last resort the long-range problem of Communist China can surely be approached better, not by building a bigger and better European super-power from the Atlantic to the Urals but by specific co-operation in different domains. Not the least object of this whole line of approach is after all precisely to soften the crystallization of the world into sharply defined power blocs and indeed, more corrosively, to change the very nature of power and responsibility in the world.

Select Bibliography

The student will obviously wish to have at his elbow the texts of the three Community Treaties, all published in English by HMSO in 1962, available also in the United Nations Treaty Series as I 3729 (Vol. 261, p. 140) and I 4300–01 (Vol. 298, pp. 11 and 169) and in other (sometimes rather corrupt) versions. The annual general reports of the three executives bring the reader up to date on developments during the year in question from the point of view of the executives concerned. The documents and proceedings of the European Parliament are published regularly, as is a welter of other material obtainable through the Communities' Press and Information Services (23 Chesham Street, London S.W.1; 808 Farragut Bdg, Farragut Square, Washington 6, D.C.).

The *Journal of Common Market Studies* (Blackwells, Oxford) devotes itself regularly to the political, legal, economic and social aspects of the Communities, and also to the comparative study of economic integration; it contains detailed up-to-date bibliographies to supplement the present highly selective list, as well as a register of current research into Common Market matters. Other articles frequently appear in *International Organization, The World Today* and *The Economist,* to mention only three of the periodicals that show a special interest in the field. *Planning* (published by Political and Economic Planning in London) from time to time has an issue on recent developments in some specific sector of Common Market affairs: PEP has also published a most useful series of Occasional Papers of the same character; and is now issuing a new series of valuable studies in conjunction with the Royal Institute of International Affairs.

Among the many recent books available in English the student may find the following the most helpful:

As a general introduction and a statement of arguments for British entry:

UWE KITZINGER, *The Challenge of the Common Market* (Basil Blackwell. Pp. 240. 12s. 6d.) 4th edn. 1962; American version *The Politics and Economics of European Integration—Britain, Europe and the United States* (Praeger. Pp. 246. $2.25) 1963.

This should be balanced by:

218

WILLIAM PICKLES, *Not With Europe: the Political Case for Staying Out* (Fabian International Bureau. Pp. 40. 3*s.* 6*d.*) 1962 or his later *Britain and Europe How much has changed?* Blackwell Pp. 119. 10*s.* 6*d.* 1967.

The most up-to-date discussion between writers of different persuasions is at the time of going to press to be found in the manuscript of a series of Third Programme broadcasts to be published under the title *Britain and the Common Market* by BBC Publications in summer 1967.

Primarily for economics students one might suggest:

BELA A. BALASSA, *The Theory of Economic Integration* (Allen & Unwin. Pp. 304. $7.35) 1962.

SIDNEY DELL, *Trade Blocs and Common Markets* (Alfred A. Knopf. Constable. Pp. 396. $5.95. 25*s.*) 1963.

JAMES E. MEADE, H. H. LIESNER & S. J. WELLS, *Case Studies in European Economic Union: the Mechanics of Integration* (Oxford University Press. pp. 424. 38*s.*) 1962.

The history of Britain's relations with Europe is told by:

NORA BELOFF, *The General Says No* (Penguin. pp. 181. 3*s.* 6*d.*) 1963.

and with rather greater scope and detail by:

MIRIAM CAMPS, *Britain and the European Community* (Oxford University Press. Princeton University Press. pp. 547. 63*s.* $8.50) 1964.

The administrative implications for Britain of integration in Europe through the fifties are discussed by:

MAX BELOFF, *New Dimensions in Foreign Policy* (Allen & Unwin. pp. 208. 25*s.*) 1961.

The more detailed study of the political process inside the Communities appears to be the preserve of American writers, particularly:

WILLIAM DIEBOLD, Jr. *The Schuman Plan—A Study in Economic Co-operation 1950–1959* (Oxford University Press., Praeger. Pp. 750. 57*s.* 6*d.* $6.50) 1959.

ERNST B. HAAS, *The Uniting of Europe* (Stevens & Sons. pp. 552. 55*s.*) 1958.

LEON N. LINDBERG, *The Political Dynamics of European Economic Integration* (Oxford University Press., Stanford University Press. pp. 367. $7.75) 1963.

Suggested Exercises

1. How far do the motivations and the forces making for West European unity twenty years ago still operate today? What new factors have arisen during this period to help and to hinder the movement for West European unity?

2. How far have the latent contradictions within the European movement disappeared or been accentuated over the past twenty years?

3. In what sense can the draft treaties for a European Defence and a European Political Community be called federal?

4. Analyse the rival drafts for a treaty of Political Union explaining the difference in underlying philosophy and the reasons for the detailed divergences in the texts.

5. To what extent is qualified majority voting essential to the working of the European Economic Community?

6. To what extent is European parliamentary control compatible with decision-making by a Council of national ministers?

7. Discuss the relationship between the two issues of West European integration and German re-unification.

8. How far do the obstacles to Britain's entry into the EEC as felt in 1961–2 still obtain today? What new difficulties have become apparent since then?

9. What is meant by describing Europe as 'inward' or 'outward-looking'? What evidence would be relevant to substantiate or controvert assertions on this subject?

10. Examine the allegation that the association between African countries and EEC is a piece of 'neo-colonialism'.

11. To what extent may groups of developing countries find it politically and economically more difficult (and in what ways may they find it easier) than Western Europe to embark on schemes of political and/or economic integration?

12. Assuming that extensive American ownership and management of European industry would speed up the rise in European

living standards, what justification is there for hostility to such 'Americanization'?

13. Does the 'Community spirit' imply among its political aims a common European nuclear force?

14. How would you define the difference between the concepts of an Atlantic partnership and an Atlantic Community?

15. Discuss the difficulties of co-ordinating regional and functional organizations within the United Nations structure.

Index